IMMIGRANT HEALTH
ENHANCING INTEGRATION & GLOBAL WELLNESS

Immigrant Health is Also Available in

Arabic as

صحة المهاجرين: تعزيز التكامل والعافية العالمية

German as *Gesundheit von Einwanderern:*
Verbesserung der Integration und des globalen Wohlbefindens

Spanish as *Salud del inmigrante:*
Mejorando la integración y el bienestar global

Other Books in the
Immigrant Strides Toward Prosperity Series

Immigrant Concepts: Life Paths to Integration

Immigrant Psychology: Health, Mind, and Soul

IMMIGRANT HEALTH

ENHANCING INTEGRATION & GLOBAL WELLNESS

Joachim O. F. Reimann, Ph.D.
Dolores I. Rodríguez-Reimann, Ph.D.

Romo Books

Immigrant Health: Enhancing Integration & Global Wellness
©2024, Joachim O. F. Reimann and Dolores I. Rodríguez-Reimann.

All rights reserved.
Published by Romo Books, Chula Vista, California

ISBN 978-1-955658-16-4 (paperback)
ISBN 978-1-955658-17-1 (eBook)
Library of Congress Control Number: 2024902040

Publisher's Cataloging-in-Publication
(Provided by Cassidy Cataloguing Services, Inc.)

Names:	Reimann, Joachim O. F., author. | Rodríguez-Reimann, Dolores Isabel, author.
Title:	Immigrant health : enhancing integration & global wellness / Joachim O.F. Reimann, Ph.D. [and] Dolores I. Rodríguez-Reimann, Ph.D.
Description:	Chula Vista, California : Romo Books, [2024] | Series: [Immigrant strides toward prosperity] | Includes bibliographical references and index.
Identifiers:	ISBN: 978-1-955658-16-4 (paperback) | 978-1-955658-17-1 (ebook) | LCCN: 2024902040
Subjects:	LCSH: Immigrants--Health and hygiene. | Immigrants--Medical care. | Immigrants--Mental health. | Emigration and immigration--Health aspects. | BISAC: SOCIAL SCIENCE / Emigration & Immigration. | HEALTH & FITNESS / Mental Health. | HEALTH & FITNESS / Diseases & Conditions / General. | PSYCHOLOGY / Mental Health.
Classification:	LCC: RA448.5.I44 R45 2024 | DDC: 362.1086912--dc23

Publishing consultant: David Wogahn, AuthorImprints.com

For our patients, colleagues, and all who
work every day on the front lines to do
their part in welcoming the stranger.

CONTENTS

PREFACE

This volume is the third and last in our series on immigrant health and adaptation to new environments. Our first book, *Immigrant Concepts: Life Paths to Integration,* provides a general overview of elements that are important to successful integration. These include occupational transitions, cultural adjustments, fostering resilience, and related areas. Our second book, *Immigrant Psychology: Heart, Mind, and Soul,* takes a more in-depth look at immigrants' psychological circumstances. This focuses on the difficulties they often face and the personal strengths they already tend to possess. Excerpts from these two books are provided at the end of this volume.

While it would help to be familiar with our other two books, the one you are reading can serve as a stand-alone text. Here we focus on public health circumstances especially relevant to immigrants. This again includes personal strengths and challenges. We then make suggestions as to how immigrants and those who work with them can foster better health and wellness.

Migration brings difficulties for both the immigrants and their new countries. Those from impoverished backgrounds need more assistance to establish themselves. But over the longer term, immigrants also make major contributions that help drive the economic engines of their adopted homes. The resulting benefits last for generations. Authors Ran Abramitzky and Leah Boustan[1] have, for example, shown that the children of immigrants in the US generally advance their economic status over their parents. This trend has been remarkably consistent since the 1880s. In short, immigration can infuse considerable vitality into a country. It can also fill critical needs. In recent years immigrant doctors, nurses, and other healthcare professionals have, for example, helped battle the COVID-19 pandemic in many countries across the globe.[2,3] In the US, in nations that are European Union members, and in other places immigrants have also been essential workers that maintained their adopted country's vital infrastructure.[4,5]

At the same time, immigration presents public health challenges. It almost goes without saying that a person's well-being is core to a happy and successful life. Yet some immigrants face hardships maintaining (and in some cases re-gaining) their health and wellness. Migrations can also introduce new health challenges to a country's native populations. Here are a few historical examples:

The story of migration's effect on various infectious diseases is long and complex. History recalls that smallpox and possibly measles were brought to Europe by Roman troops who had fought in Western Asia.[6] It is also thought that the Huns brought the Justinian Plague to Europe, the Near East, and other regions around 541 AD. This plague may have killed as many as 25 million people.[7]

In addition, Western explorers introduced smallpox and measles into Pacific Island nations. American settlers in the "new world" also introduced multiple diseases including smallpox, cholera, scarlet fever, and whooping cough to Native tribes.[8] It is estimated that this contributed to a Native American population decline within current US borders from roughly 600,000 in 1800 to about 250,000 in 1900.

More recently migrations have been associated with the spread of COVID-19 and monkeypox (aka Mpox) among other illnesses.[9] This has, in part, been facilitated by our global economy's ability to routinely move people and goods faster through technological advances in shipping and air travel.[10,11]

How do we respond to such trends? Given increasingly connected countries, travel is essential. Economic growth is unlikely if we were to just stand still. The resulting stagnation would likely trigger higher unemployment and other unwanted results. In short, migrations need to and will continue to occur. Such realities prompted us to write this book.

We start by discussing examples of the illnesses and other health challenges some immigrants can be exposed to in their country of origin or while migrating.

We then provide examples of the unique circumstances around health that some immigrants face in their new country. This includes common illnesses that many people get, but that immigrants may be less familiar with. It also includes illnesses and accidents that immigrants are more at risk for in their new homes. In this discussion, we address the connections between psychological and physical health.

The book also talks about circumstances immigrants often encounter when they seek healthcare in their new country. This includes contacts with doctors and other providers, realistic and unrealistic expectations of patients, and whether the services immigrants receive will be effective. The discussion includes how acculturation impacts people's ideas about health and illness as well as their ability to access adequate care. We also review some financial circumstances involved in healthcare insurance. Additionally, we address differences between medications and other treatments people are accustomed to in their country of origin and those available in their new homes. Specifically, medications (both prescription and over-the-counter) and remedies that people routinely take in their country of origin may not exist (or may not be legal) in their adopted country. Rohypnol (Flunitrazepam), for example, is an especially potent anti-anxiety agent in the family called benzodiazepines (like Xanax and Valium). It is used in parts of Europe, Japan, Australia, South Africa, and Latin America. But it is not approved for medical use in the US.[12]

How do we improve worldwide healthcare? The COVID-19 pandemic has been a highly disruptive event in many of our lives. But this pandemic can also teach us how to do better when similar incidents happen in the future. Most fundamentally, we need to address the global context of disease. Viruses and bacteria do not respect international borders. They go where humans (and in some instances the animals they infect) allow them to go. Given the interconnectedness of the world, we expect that infectious diseases will spread more easily and create new pandemics in the future. This will require an international understanding of disease transmission and the coordinated management of resources to combat illness.

As such, there is a need for countries and their healthcare systems to better organize their efforts. That includes ideas about how to accomplish effective multinational disease management. Areas of consideration, for example, involve global efforts to develop and distribute vaccines and treatments, acceptance of needed providers with foreign education and training, disease prevention campaigns, and the use of social media in constructive ways.

We also spend some time reviewing wellness through the dietary changes immigrants may encounter in new countries, immigrants' ability to organize and advocate for themselves in accessing healthcare, how they can use spirituality to foster health and related topics. While our discussion is not comprehensive, we hope it provides basic examples that will spark readers' interest to learn more. As in our other books, we present examples from our work and personal experiences that highlight certain points we cover.

It may seem that some of our examples, at first glance, do not make a major impact. However, it is important to recognize that even small differences in healthcare practices between countries can sow confusion. One such example is the case of the Bacillus Calmette–Guerin (BCG) vaccine, most commonly used outside the US to prevent Tuberculosis. It can cause a false positive reaction in a purified protein derivative (PPD) skin test for TB.[13]

Who is our audience? There are times when we address immigrants directly. At other points, our comments are more specifically directed at healthcare workers. This is intentional. Both will need to understand each other, work together, and jointly advocate for improvements in care.

In short, issues of health and wellness present challenges for many who have left their country of origin. We hope that this book will encourage people to seek the care they need and deserve. Ironically, wellness can also be contagious. Our neighbor's good health increases the chance that we will be healthy as well.

Readers may find the initial chapters in this volume more technical. We need to present numbers on the scope of problems immigrants tend to face. The latter part then presents practical advice for both immigrants and those working with them.

DISCLAIMER

The content presented in this book is only meant for public health education and reference purposes. It reflects the opinions, perspectives, and experiences of the authors. This book should not be seen as a substitute for professional advice given by a physician or other licensed healthcare providers. You should not use this information to self-diagnose or try to treat any illnesses or other medical conditions. Please contact a healthcare provider immediately if you suspect that you have a medical problem.

Efforts have been made to provide information and statements that are accurate and consistent with formal peer-reviewed research and other credible sources. These are referenced throughout the book.

CONDITIONS IMMIGRANTS EXPERIENCE IN THEIR COUNTRY OF ORIGIN AND/ OR ENCOUNTER EN ROUTE

Immigrants come from very diverse backgrounds and circumstances. The media tends to cover those who are forced to flee danger. But many people also move to a new country because they are highly sought after. They bring advanced skills and expertise and are essentially "imported." In the US there are specialized visas (H-1B and O-1) for people in a variety of fields who have extraordinary abilities with comparable education. Some of these mechanisms do not automatically grant permanent residence but do allow for extended stays.[14]

We recognize that even people in such positions tend to experience stress as they face migration challenges. Their circumstances are discussed at various points in this book. But migrants with fewer economic means and those who seek to escape various dangers tend to face the greatest health challenges. Consequently, much of our book addresses such groups.

The United Nations' Institute of Migration (IOM) reports that there were 281 million international migrants worldwide in 2020. Of these, 89.4. million were displaced due to war, persecution, other violence, and disasters.[15] Where do people migrate from? They often come from Central and Southern

Asia, Latin America and the Caribbean, Northern Africa, and the greater Middle East.[16]

It probably comes as a surprise that, while Europe and Northern America take in the greatest number of immigrants, these regions are also the origin of many people who migrate to other countries such as Canada as well as Central and South America.

As previously noted, people migrate for various reasons. These include better career opportunities, escape from war, persecution, other dangers, and changes in country conditions. One example that has arguably received too little attention is global warming - even though it has been connected with human migrations, particularly over the past two centuries. Global warming refers to increases in the Earth's surface temperatures over time. It has been linked to both "natural" events (such as volcanic eruptions) as well human activities. Causes related to our human population include 1) commercial deforestation, 2) motor vehicle emissions (carbon dioxide and other toxins), 3) chlorofluorocarbons (chemicals used in air conditioners and refrigerators that affect our planet's protective ozone layer), 4) overall industrial development, 5) agricultural practices that create carbon dioxide and methane gas, and 6) general overpopulation.[17]

In part, global warming is thought to increase flooding, fires, droughts, and storms. It has also resulted in rising sea levels. The latter has caused whole Pacific islands to disappear underwater or become otherwise uninhabitable (an example is the Republic of Kiribati). Climate change has also caused famine and other human suffering. In addition, increased temperatures can aid disease transmission. Mosquitos and tics thrive in warmer climates, raising the chances that people will contract malaria and other illnesses.[18]

Not surprisingly such conditions can lead people to seek safety by moving elsewhere. This is sometimes referred to as environmental migration. In 2017 alone, an estimated 22.5 to 24 million people were displaced by events caused by climate change.[19,20] Many of them come from Latin America, sub-Saharan Africa, and Southeast Asia.

Though critically important, it bears repeating that climate change is just one of many difficulties prompting migrations. Many of these challenges can be traced to the country's conditions at home. This chapter discusses specific examples illustrating the point.

DEVELOPMENTAL IMPAIRMENTS

Immigrants fleeing violent, impoverished, or other problematic conditions at home have often experienced poor sanitation that fosters disease, a lack of available healthcare, and other instabilities. Given their critical time of growth, children are especially prone to difficulties that can last a lifetime. The World Health Organization (WHO), for example, uses a term called "stunting" and defines it as *impaired growth and development that children experience from poor nutrition, repeated infection, and inadequate psychosocial stimulation.*[21] One major factor prompting "stunting" is food insecurity.

It comes as no surprise that children who are well-nourished with a balanced diet are more likely to be healthy, productive, and able to learn. Conversely, malnutrition has been associated with reduced intellect, low productivity, greater vulnerability to disease, and an eventual life of poverty.

As we write this book news headlines focus on a number of places where food insecurity is a significant and potentially worsening problem. Addressing Afghanistan after the 2021

Taliban takeover, for example, a UNICEF report[22] notes that the country has one of the world's highest malnutrition rates. One in three adolescent girls is anemic and only 12 percent of Afghan children aged 6-24 months receive the right variety and amount of food they need for their age.

At 41%, Afghanistan has one of the world's highest rates of stunting in children. Food is scarce and sometimes children are forced to have a diet that is low in nutrition and high in contaminants. The COVID-19 pandemic and political instability have contributed to these problems. The result is that children are at greater risk of developing diarrhea, pneumonia, and other health problems.

Syria is another country where food insecurity is a major and increasing problem. In addition to that country's civil war, a 2019 economic crisis in neighboring Lebanon, combined with the COVID-19 pandemic, a severe drought that is ongoing as we write this book, a fuel scarcity that reduces the ability to operate wells, and declining humanitarian aid have all contributed to food shortages.[23] The World Food Programme[24] thus estimates that nearly 60% of Syria's population is now food insecure.[25]

Other places with food insecurity are as follows: According to the 2021 Global Hunger Index countries with some of the greatest malnutrition risk by region are West and North Africa (Yemen and Iraq), West Africa (Liberia and Sierra Leone), Central and Southern Africa (the Central African Republic and Chad), East Africa (Somalia and Madagascar), South America (Venezuela), Central America and the Caribbean (Haiti and Guatemala) and Southeast Asia (Timor-Leste and Afghanistan). In Europe and Central Asia Turkmenistan is listed.

(Turkmenistan's hunger index is not, however, designated as problematic).[26]

Not surprisingly, there is some overlap between food insecurity and home countries from which most migrants in the world seek to escape. As per World Vision,[27] these include Syria (6.8 million refugees), Venezuela (5.4 million refugees), Afghanistan (2.8 million refugees), and Somalia (800,000 refugees) to name a few.

OTHER CONDITIONS PREVALENT IN COUNTRIES OF ORIGIN

One focus of research has been the prevalence of certain diseases among developing countries. In such environments, the combination of poverty, malnutrition, weak infrastructure (e.g., poor sewage disposal), and few medical services often leads to greater severity and transmission of various infectious diseases than found in other places. This has a particular impact on vulnerable populations such as the elderly.

Leading causes of death in developing countries before the COVID-19 pandemic were non-COVID-19 respiratory tract infections and illnesses causing diarrhea, tuberculosis, and malaria. Together these diseases accounted for more than 90% of deaths among the elderly.[28] We discuss several illnesses and conditions in greater detail below.

Infectious Diseases

COVID-19: Not surprisingly, the most severe recent health crisis has been prompted by the COVID-19 pandemic. As we are writing this book it has spread to 228 countries and has caused almost 6.5 million deaths.[29] These numbers are growing daily. While effective vaccines and treatments have been developed, new variants continue to appear, and some people continue to distrust medical solutions. This challenges healthcare's progress in bringing the disease under long-term control.

The pandemic has required various social groups, including immigrants, to consider changing common practices. For example, in the US more immigrants live in multigenerational households than the broader population.[30] In such homes, family members from three or more age groups live together. Under most conditions, multigenerational households can be helpful. They have the potential to strengthen family bonds, make childcare and elder care easier, and help save money.[31] Studies have also found that, among West Indian and Latin American immigrant groups, multigenerational households help increase homeownership and emotional support among family members.[32] This practice has, however, created problems during the COVID-19 pandemic. Consistent and close contact between family members increases the risk of disease transmission.[33] Thus the COVID-19 pandemic households have faced new health challenges that require them to adapt.

In addition, COVID-19 has highlighted that a pandemic impacts the worldwide economy as well as healthcare systems and individuals. It has disrupted manufacturing, supply lines, and many other enterprises. Service businesses such as restaurants and gyms have had to adapt to restrictions that limit COVID-19 spread or cease operating altogether. The International Monetary Fund has estimated that the overall global gross domestic product (GDP) dropped by 3.9% from 2019 to 2020 alone.[34] Immigrants have both affected and been impacted by COVID-19 in various ways. Some immigrants from African and Latin American ethnic/racial groups have had greater infection rates than the general population. In part, this is likely caused by the type of work they often perform. As we will discuss later, such trends may be fostered by their frequent participation in service occupations that have been designated as essential and involve greater public contact.[35] It is notable that this type of contact includes work in direct-service healthcare occupations. In other words, immigrants are often at greater risk of contracting COVID-19 but also contribute to society's battle against the disease.

Interactions between infectious diseases and migration are nothing new. Sometimes even diseases we believe have been defeated by medications and other treatments suddenly make a comeback. Examples include tuberculosis, leishmaniasis (a parasitic infection spread by sandflies), and helminthiasis (a worm infection). Here is a more specific discussion about tuberculosis:

Tuberculosis: As per the World Health Organization's 2021 data tuberculosis (TB) is the 13th leading overall cause of death and the second leading infectious killer after COVID-19. This bacterial infection primarily attacks the lungs but can spread to other parts of the body. In the past, it was also called consumption. Without proper treatment, up to two-thirds of people with TB die.[36]

Once thought to be almost completely eradicated with medications (antibiotics), TB made a comeback in the 1980s and 1990s.[37,38] Unfortunately, TB remains a significant problem. Worldwide roughly 1.6 million people died from the disease in 2021.[36]

Historically, TB has been of concern along some international borders. A 2018 overview article explored immigration and TB in the US. It concluded that overall, TB rates are highest among people who were not born in the US. Fortunately, a more detailed analysis over time shows that the rates are declining among people who have immigrated to the US from Mexico, South Korea, Ecuador, and Peru. Rates among those from the Philippines, India, Ethiopia, and Honduras have largely remained unchanged. Rates among those originating from China have slightly increased.[39] It is thus important to understand and focus on trends in disease transmission over time. We don't need to fear one population for importing presumed health risks. We do need to understand that individuals, healthcare, and governments can take steps to mitigate illness.

Other groups at risk for TB include migrant farm workers. But, notably, this group has higher rates of latent (no longer infectious) TB.[40] In our own research, we have found cultural factors that influence Mexican Americans' decision to seek medical TB prevention services. We will cover our findings in a later section of this book.

One 2020 study addressing TB impact of immigration on countries in the European Union (EU) showed mixed results. It found no overall connection between immigration and higher TB rates. In fact, some countries with more immigrants actually had fewer TB cases. But this trend is not universal. Contrary to the general findings, Italy, Germany, and Norway have shown more incidents of TB connected with immigration.[41] The reason for this observation is uncertain. But it is probably connected to the number of immigrants who come from countries with high TB infection rates.

It is notable that some countries will not allow migrants with certain diseases to come into the country. People seeking to enter the US, for example, undergo a medical evaluation. Those with infectious diseases including active untreated TB, syphilis, gonorrhea, and Hansen's disease are not allowed to enter. But those who have completed successful TB treatment in another country, those who have symptoms similar to TB but for which a current TB infection has been ruled out, and those who have a latent TB infection can still be allowed to come in. Medical follow-up in these cases may be required.[42] In addition, the US imposed temporary restrictions on the immigration process in response to the COVID-19 pandemic. For example, until recently a US policy (called the Title 42 authority) was used to turn away migrants, including asylum seekers at the US–Mexico border, under the assumption that they could worsen the COVID-19 pandemic.[43]

Trauma

Many refugees have experienced physical and emotional trauma, both in their country of origin and while migrating. Traumatic incidents are often caused by war, torture, assault (including sexual assault), and accidents during difficult journeys. One study conducted in a Turkish Emergency Department, for example, found that Syrian refugees presented with much greater incidents of head injury, fractures, skin injuries, and burns than the native population.[44] Research conducted in Lebanon also found that injuries were most commonly sustained by children and younger adults (up to 45 years of age) and included stabbings, gunshots, and concussions.[45] In our own clinical experience with East African refugees, having been hit over the head with an AK-47 rifle butt during a home invasion by assailants is routinely described by our patients.

Sexual assault is another horrendous trend that has, in some cases, become a weapon of war and terror. In Ukraine invading Russian troops have, for example, been accused of raping both girls and boys as young as one year of age as well as men and women who are in their 70s or older. Incidents of gang rape and circumstances in which loved ones are forced to watch sexually violent acts against a partner or child have been cited. It is further reported that a one-year-old boy died as a result of such an assault.[46,47]

Notes from the UN Security Council also report that criminal organizations are taking advantage of social instabilities during the war to conduct human trafficking operations that include children.[48] Women who believe they are responding to legitimate employment offers are ultimately forced into the sex trade.

Exploiting vulnerable women is hardly new. Historically, women and girls have been pressed into sex slavery by terrorist groups such as Boko Haram in Nigeria, the Islamic State (ISIS) in Syria and other locations.[49]

Aside from the psychological terror this causes, some people, especially young children, are left with physical injuries. Child physiology is simply not developed enough to tolerate intercourse. In addition, some people are intentionally injured as an intimidation technique during sexual assaults. The consequences are frequently called anogenital injuries (AGI) and can require surgery.[50]

Some medical illnesses can be thought of as a byproduct of war. For example, refugees from Syria have exhibited higher rates of respiratory disease. This is thought to be caused by chemicals and dust thrown up by military attacks.[51]

In addition, a country at war on its own turf often loses the infrastructure necessary to treat illnesses and injuries. Tahir-begolli and colleagues, for example, report that in some Syrian cities children and youth have often not received preventive care (such as vaccines) which leaves them vulnerable to diseases including measles and polio.[51] As in the case of Afghanistan cited earlier, health problems are further exacerbated by food shortages, malnutrition, and a lack of safe housing. This again, makes both children and adults more vulnerable to disease and death.

As we write this book the Russian invasion of Ukraine continues. The World Health Organization (WHO) reports that this has severely degraded Ukraine's healthcare infrastructure while the need for medical help for both military and civilian wounded has increased dramatically.

Dr. Hans Henri Kluge, the WHO's Regional Director for Europe has further said that there were 260 verified direct attacks on healthcare in Ukraine during the first 100 days of the war.[52] A similar pattern was noted during Syria's civil war. In 2017 the Soufan Center estimated that, at the time, Syrian government forces alone had killed almost 700 medical personnel throughout the country.[53] It was believed that some providers and hospitals were specifically targeted, probably with the intent to demoralize and subjugate the local population.

OTHER HEALTH FACTORS

Oral health is often overlooked in discussions about immigrants. Yet, on average, migrants' oral health is known to be worse than a country's native population.[54] Problems include dental cavities, tooth loss, and infections.

This trend may be true because people feel that other medical issues require more immediate attention and access to dentists is restricted by financial resources (e.g., no dental insurance) as well as limited provider availability.[55] But over the long run dental disease can result in tooth and bone loss. Infections from tooth decay can also spread through the bloodstream. Severe dental infections can move beyond the jawbone and into the neck and other areas. In extreme cases, infections can create blood clots in hollow spaces under the brain and behind each eye socket (cavernous sinus thrombosis) that have other major consequences and can even be life-threatening.[56] So, while it may not seem so, maintaining oral health is important.

RISKS WHILE MIGRATING

For migrants with few economic means, the journey to a new country can entail a multiplicity of hazards. Health risks include exposure to disease, accidents, exacerbation of existing health problems in the process of traveling and being a victim of violence, including sexual assault.

While addressing information from Europe, the World Health Organization identified accidental injuries, hypothermia, gastrointestinal illnesses, burns, cardiovascular events, diabetes, and hypertension as some of the most frequent problems among newly arrived immigrants and refugees.[57] Poor hygiene while traveling can also lead to skin and parasite infections. Women often face pregnancy and childbirth-related issues as well as exposure to violence. Here are some specific dangers.

Dangers

Traumatic experiences do not only happen in the country of a migrant's origin. They're also acquired in the process of traveling where accidents are another all-too-frequent occurrence. The United Nations High Commissioner for Refugees (UNHCR) for example, has reported that 3,100 refugees crossing the Mediterranean Sea are thought to have died or gone missing in the first 10 months of 2015 alone.[58] Another 938 were believed dead or missing during the first half of 2022.[59]

Migrants traveling from South and Central America to the US-Mexico Border also face a multitude of hazards. For example, many walk through the Darién Gap, a roughly 60-mile stretch of dense rainforest between Colombia and Panama. This trek is without roads and includes treacherous mountains and swamps. It is thought to be one of the most dangerous migration routes in the world. Many migrants seeking entry to the US then travel through Mexico on top of a freight train colloquially called *La Bestia* (the beast) or *El tren de la muerte* (the train of death). These nicknames are well-earned. Dangers include accidents as people jump onto and off the moving train. In addition, migrants sometimes fall asleep, are shaken off due to the train's movement, land on the tracks, and are killed.[60] Since these accidents often occur at night and in rural areas when people are sleeping, others do not immediately know that anything has happened. In addition, migrants riding this train tend to be the victims of violence, robberies, and kidnappings.[61,62]

Dangers can continue once immigrants reach the country they seek to enter. For example, on June 27, 2022, sixty-four migrants were found in an abandoned truck in San Antonio, Texas. Ultimately 53 of them died, most likely due to dehydration and heat. This incident has been described as the deadliest human smuggling case in modern US history. The deceased had come from Mexico, Guatemala, and Honduras. They ranged in age from 13 to 55 years.[63]

In April of 2021, a report by the Houston Texas television station, KTRK, also described an incident in which police investigated an alleged kidnapping. It turned out to be a human smuggling operation. Ninety people were found huddled inside one residence. Of these, five people tested positive for COVID-19. The police then began to administer rapid tests when others said they could not smell or taste anything (a hallmark symptom of the virus).[64]

2

RISKS AND OTHER CIRCUMSTANCES IMMIGRANTS FACE AT THEIR DESTINATION

Immigrants, like their native-born counterparts, are routinely susceptible to various illnesses, often developing the same illnesses as the native population. Some researchers have however noted that heart disease and cancer occur less frequently among immigrants than in a country's broader population.[65] But certain circumstances can have a more specific impact on health and safety. One such arena is the workplace.

Industrial Injuries: Workers with a migrant background in Germany are often exposed to more physical stress and difficult conditions than their native counterparts.[66] The same is true in other countries including Italy, the US, and Canada. Newly arrived immigrants are more likely to work in dangerous jobs and are thus more likely to be injured. This includes exposure to heat, pesticides, potentially harmful chemicals, and other hazards that can cause industrial accidents.[67,68]

A recent example that gained media attention involved the hazards immigrant workers experienced as the prepared venues for Qatar's 2022 World Cup events. This included building stadiums as well as infrastructure such as new roads, hotels, a new public transportation system, and an airport expansion. To complete the projects Qatar hired many foreign workers, most often from Nepal, Bangladesh, India, Pakistan, and Sri Lanka.

These workers passed health screenings before gaining a Qatari visa. So, initial poor health was presumably not a problem. But then a substantial number of workers died throughout their employment. Specific figures are hard to determine but were estimated at around 6,500 by *The Guardian*.[69] *Deutsche Welle* (DW)[70] notes that this estimate is too high. But Qatari officials have acknowledged that between 400 and 500 workers connected with World Cup projects died.[71] In addition, others reportedly passed away from conditions such as kidney failure after returning to their country of origin. This has been linked to conditions such as hot weather and poor drinking water people experienced in Qatar.[72]

Who is generally most susceptible to an industrial injury? A study from Spain showed that immigrants from North Africa were at particular risk. Working North African women suffered the most burns from industrial accidents. Men from Latin America, the Caribbean, Africa, and Eastern Europe most often suffered foreign object injuries (e.g., being hit by an object, getting something in the eye, or swallowing things by accident).[73] Not surprisingly, research has found that immigrants in high-risk jobs are more likely to develop chronic pain than the general population.[74]

Comment by Joachim Reimann

In my clinical practice I routinely perform evaluations with people who have had industrial injuries and are thus involved in California's Workers' Compensation System. Most such people have psychological difficulties due to a physical on-the-job accident. During the years 2021 and 2022, I saw 22 clients with such conditions. Of those, 15 had Spanish surnames. Most were born in Mexico and five did not speak English. Two of the remaining clients were from Southeast Asia.

While this is not a scientific sample, it does illustrate the frequency with which immigrants are hurt during the course of employment compared to other populations. In addition, negotiating the Workers' Compensation System can be complex. This can make it hard for injured workers, especially those who do not speak English, to get the timely services they need. A treatment delay tends to increase the probability that conditions become chronic and require more intensive care. In short, the process can increase both human suffering and ultimate monetary costs.

Diabetes: Differences in eating habits can also alter immigrants' health status. For example, people with African, Latin American, Pacific Island, and Asian backgrounds are especially susceptible to developing type 2 diabetes.[75] Why might this be true?

People who are overweight, older, or have an immediate family member with type 2 diabetes are particularly susceptible to contracting the disease. One idea why some ethnic groups are at such risk is known as the "thrifty genotype" hypothesis.[76] The assumption states that certain groups may have genes that help increase their body's fat storage. In environments where access to nutritious diets is limited, this would have advantages. It would allow people to effectively store fat when food is more available so they can rely on that fat in times of famine. The process would be particularly helpful for child-bearing women.

But when immigrants from these environments reach new countries in which food is consistently abundant and more processed, the thrifty genotype can create problems. It essentially prepares for a famine that never comes. This is thought to foster chronic obesity and related health problems like diabetes.

The thrifty genotype hypothesis has been criticized for a number of reasons. There is, for example, concern that it minimizes our ability to take responsibility for our own health through making good dietary choices.[77] In our view, this is not an "either-or" question. Genetics, our actions around food, and our physical activity levels all impact our health.

Specifically, there is evidence that eating healthy food and exercising does work. The Diabetes Prevention Program (DPP), a large and important study, found that lifestyle changes decreased the number of people developing type 2 diabetes by 58%.[78] This finding means that even people with genetic factors making them more susceptible to certain diseases can also significantly reduce that risk by making healthy choices.

Overall, the notable type 2 diabetes rates among immigrants are probably driven by a number of circumstances. In addition to the thrifty genotype, immigrants sometimes gain weight due to stress which develops into a habit of self-soothing anxiety with food.

INTERNATIONAL DIFFERENCES IN TOBACCO USE

Another topic is tobacco use. Smoking and related tobacco use are major health problems. The World Health Organization reports that tobacco products, directly and indirectly, kill more than 8 million people a year worldwide.[79] This includes roughly 1.2 million deaths linked to second-hand smoke.[80]

Tobacco use involves different products including cigarettes, cigars, chewing tobacco (dip, snuff), dissolvable tobacco, shisha (which combines tobacco and fruit or vegetable products that are smoked using a hookah), and pipe tobacco. As discussed in more detail below, immigrants are likely to encounter unfamiliar tobacco use patterns in their adopted countries as such patterns vary and change over time.

Changing Tobacco Use Patterns: There are times when a specific tobacco product becomes especially popular. For example, the 25-year US decline in cigar smoking suddenly reversed in 1991. A growing number of social events, internet sites, and bars celebrated cigars. Trendy models smoking cigars appeared on magazine covers. Our own research at the time showed that Latinos were among the groups with high smoking rates.[81] Smokers saw cigars as a safe alternative to cigarettes because they did not inhale the smoke.[82] This perception is not accurate. Cigar use is associated with cancer of the larynx and other health risks. As per a 2020 Truth Initiative report[83] cigar smoking in the US has not declined, has in fact increased among young people, and thus continues to pose substantial health risks.

The search for a safe way of smoking continues, most recently with the advent of electronic cigarettes (E-cigarettes). These are battery-powered devices, often shaped like a cigarette, that provide the user with nicotine. While e-cigarettes do not include tobacco, the vapor they produce contains known toxins that can cause breathing problems and other health risks.[84]

Societal norms and tobacco use: Some products people smoke are associated with specific countries and cultures. For example, kreteks (also referred to as clove cigarettes) come from Indonesia. Hookah (water) pipes are thought to have been developed in India and became especially popular in the Middle East.

Tobacco use can thus vary widely from nation to nation. World Population Review 2022 statistics cite Nauru (52.10%), Kiribati (52.00%), Tuvalu (48.70%), Myanmar (45.50%), Chile (44.70%), Lebanon (42.60%), Serbia (40.60%), Bangladesh (39.10%), Greece (39.10%), and Bulgaria (38.90%) as the ten countries with the highest smoking rates.[85]

Smoking rates within EU member countries vary greatly from the previously cited high in Greece to a low of 7% in Sweden.[86] The US year 2020 cigarette smoking rates were estimated at 12.5%.[87]

How do such numbers relate to immigrants? Research has shown that culture influences tobacco use in a variety of ways. One US study, for example, found that immigrants from Arab nations who continued to follow their country of origin's norms were more likely to smoke cigarettes or hookah pipes than others in their communities.[88] Conversely, research from Australia showed that people who had immigrated there from non-English-speaking countries were less likely to smoke than the local population. But those who had arrived as children or adolescents were then more likely to smoke than native-born Australians after they had been in the country for 20 years or more.[89] In short, smoking patterns depend on a variety of customs in immigrants' countries of origin and the circumstances where they now live.

Example, Joachim's father:
Given that smoking is linked with a multitude of health problems, continuing the habit is never a good idea. A few people find quitting easy. When Joachim's father immigrated from Germany to the US, he was mildly annoyed that his usual brand of cigarette (HB) was not

locally available. So, he just stopped smoking. But we suspect that quitting is more difficult than that for most habitual smokers. They may need nicotine replacement therapy (such as patches), social support, and other methods to help them achieve that goal. The good news is that quitting tobacco has been linked to reduced risks of developing various cancers, heart disease, stroke, and other medical problems.[90]

Questions immigrants can ask themselves about tobacco use include:

1. If tobacco use is more accepted in my new country, will I be tempted to start (or continue) such use, even if I know the health risks?
2. Is the move to an adopted country a good time to stop using tobacco, since I'm starting a kind of "new life" there?
3. If I want to quit tobacco use, what supports to help me do so are available in my new country?

INTERSECTIONS BETWEEN PHYSICAL ILLNESS AND MENTAL HEALTH

Many Western societies still tend to think of mental health and physical health as involving two different realms. This may have developed from a philosophy called mind-body dualism, often associated with the French philosopher René Descartes. Essentially this view says that the mind and body are distinct and separate.[91] The concept is found in many Western religions including Christianity. The belief holds that a differentiation exists between the body and the soul.[92] In healthcare terms, Western religious traditions often see physical illness in the realm of medicine and spiritual or psychic (and thus psychological) illness as falling under their purview. While religious authorities are in the process of rethinking this concept, mind-body dualism has had, and continues to have, a substantial influence on how healthcare systems are structured.[93]

In contrast, the philosophy shared by many Eastern traditions (such as Buddhism and Taoism) sees the body and psyche in a more holistic, fully integrated way.[94] Immigrants coming from such locations might thus be surprised by Western medicine and doubtful that it will be effective.

Some trends show that medicine is changing in the West. The World Health Organization has recognized the need for a holistic approach. Specifically, it defines health as "a state of complete physical, mental and social well-being and not merely the absence of disease or infirmity." The WHO adds "there is no health without mental health."[95]

In short, mental and physical health are fundamentally connected. Here are three specific examples that are relevant to immigrants.

Physical injury and pain: As we have previously said, some immigrants experience physical trauma at home (e.g., through war and criminal violence), in their travels (e.g., through violent exploitation and accidents), and in their adopted country because they become victims of hate crimes. Because they are more likely to work in physically demanding work, immigrants are also more likely to be injured on the job.[68,96,97] These circumstances can lead to chronic pain.

Pain is a complex topic. At present, no direct physical measure can confirm the existence and severity of an individual's pain experiences. Nevertheless, as all human beings probably know, pain is a very real and unpleasant sensation. There are several types of pain. One is called "nociceptive." This generally involves tissue damage from bruising, burns, or other injuries to a body part.[98] A second type of pain is called "neuropathic."[99] This is caused by problems with the human nervous system due to an injury or illness. Finally, some causes for pain remain unknown. For example, how conditions such as irritable bowel syndrome, fibromyalgia, and chronic headaches develop is not yet clearly understood.

Pain can be further divided into two general categories: acute and chronic. Acute pain is usually experienced as a consequence of a specific injury or illness. Examples are muscle strains, bone fractures, and kidney stones. Acute pain tends to be a short-term problem that subsides after the underlying injury has healed. In contrast, pain becomes chronic when it lasts three or more months.

In some instances, pain serves an important function. I can alert us to existing physical injuries, including those that may become worse if we do not attend to them. But in other instances, when pain becomes chronic, it does not contribute any practical benefit to our survival. In other words, such pain serves no useful function in our physical recovery. This is particularly true of neuropathic pain.[100]

It is probably no surprise that unresolved pain can cause people to become frustrated, anxious, and depressed. The combination of pain and emotional difficulties tends to worsen both conditions, making them more difficult to treat.[101,102,103]

In addition, one Canadian study focusing on immigrants showed that mood and anxiety disorders were significantly connected with a greater probability of injury, particularly those caused by falling.[104] In short, those with chronic pain are at risk of having poor mental health, and people with poor mental health are at heightened risk for physical injury.

Chronic illnesses: Chronic illnesses and emotional disturbances can also be linked. As previously described some immigrant groups are at particular risk of developing type 2 diabetes. This illness is frustrating because it takes ongoing and intensive efforts to control. People have to stick with specific diets, have exercise routines, monitor their blood sugar levels, and use other methods to avoid serious medical problems. Given the emotional toll this takes, it has been linked to depression. This is true for the general population as well as for immigrants.[105] In addition, psychological stress has been connected with physical risks for developing type 2 diabetes.[106] In other words, there can be an unfortunate cycle in which frustration and sadness about having diabetes lead to physical reactions that worsen diabetes.

In response to this problem, a number of diabetes care systems have included an emphasis on emotional well-being and personal empowerment in their approaches to diabetes care. Research shows that these efforts can yield positive results.[107,108]

Autoimmune Disorders: These are diseases that cause the body's immune system to destroy healthy body tissue by mistake. Specific diseases include those that cause problems for our joints and muscles, organs, digestion, tissues, and chronic inflammation. Researchers have found chronic stress to be one element that increases the chance of developing such a disorder.[109]

Stress should be triggered by dangerous situations in which our body releases a hormone called adrenalin to increase our blood pressure, breathing, and pulse rate. Historically this has served humans well. If they were under threat of attack by a predator or faced other life-threatening circumstances, the body adjusted to increase the chances of survival. These tend to be temporary situations in which our body calms down once we are safe. However, experiencing continuous stress in which the body releases adrenaline over a longer period of time can result in continuous inflammation and other health issues. For example, chronic stress can create a physical process that leads to type 2 diabetes.[106] In addition, research has found that stress, including posttraumatic stress disorder (PTSD), is related to the development of autoimmune disorders.[110]

Research on the connections between chronic stress and autoimmune disorders among immigrants is limited. Such links tend to vary by migrants' individual circumstances including the conditions in the country they come from.[111] But studies show clear links between Posttraumatic Stress Disorder (PTSD) and such autoimmune disorders.[112] Given relatively high PTSD rates among some immigrant groups such as refugees it makes sense to suspect that they also experience autoimmune problems.[113] In addition, African-origin and Latin American children with foreign-born parents have especially high risks of low-grade but persistent inflammation.[114] That, in turn, puts them at risk of developing autoimmunity problems.

Other Examples: There are many other circumstances in which mental and physical issues interact with each other. Frequent problems sleeping (insomnia) can, for example, contribute to the risk of developing heart disease, diabetes, and high blood pressure. Insomnia can also lead to increases in the risk of developing or worsening Alzheimer's disease, other types of dementia, as well as mood disorders such as depression, PTSD, and general anxiety.

Given the connections between emotional and physical health, the irony that we have written two separate books, one on psychological and one on physical health does not escape us. But immigrants coming to a new country may still need to understand and negotiate healthcare environments that often have separate systems for mental and physical providers and insurance coverage. Sometimes mental and physical health services are also housed in different locations. Calls to more fully integrate mental and physical health continue to be made in the scientific literature.[115]

4

PATIENT EXPERIENCES
AND EXPECTATIONS

W hen immigrants seek medical help in a new country, they will likely encounter practices that are very different from those they are accustomed to. These include the type of medications, vaccines, and treatments that are available, how and when diagnostic tests are used, and other healthcare approaches. Immigrants' reactions to these differences influence how satisfied they are with services, their confidence that the services they receive will be effective, and whether they will seek help from local providers in the future.

Next, we provide some examples of the differences in healthcare approaches and systems. This discussion is not comprehensive. But we hope it gives readers a general sense of what immigrants will probably encounter.

MEDICATIONS

Immigrants are likely to find that the laws around medication use differ from country to country. The medications they could readily buy in their home country may require a doctor's prescription or may not be readily available in the country they have migrated to. Others may be banned entirely. Some examples of banned anti-pain medications in the US are Oxyphenbutazone (trade names Tandearil and Tanderil), Nimesulide (multiple trade names including Acenim), Propoxyphene (trade name

Darvon), and Nitrofurasone (multiple trade names including Amifur).[116] The US Food and Drug Administration (FDA) has found that the potential negative side effects outweigh the benefits these medications provide.

On the other hand, some medications that are available in the US are illegal in other locations. For example, Attention-Deficit / Hyperactivity Disorder medications (e.g., Adderall, Concerta, Ritalin), pain medications such as Vicodin, and anti-anxiety benzodiazepines such as Xanax and Valium are not available in Europe. This does not mean people who are visitors to a foreign country cannot take the medications they need and are accustomed to having with them, even in the event of an extended stay.

Specialized Academic Instruction (SAI), an organization that helps US students study abroad, for example, makes the following recommendations. Some of these also apply to immigrants. In addition, people traveling through several countries to reach their destinations need to consider the laws and procedures in each one.[117]

1. Bring a full supply of the prescription medication(s) you will likely need for your time in another country. (But review other considerations below to see if that will be legal in the place you are traveling to).

2. Has your US physician provided you with a signed and dated note in English on their practice letterhead that includes the name of the medication (including the generic name and that it is not a narcotic), your full name, the amount of the medication you are bringing, and that the medication is necessary for your health (naming the specific condition)? You cannot take your medications

with you to Europe without such documentation. Other countries may not even accept that process.

3. Keep each medicine in its original packaging and bottles.
4. The packaging and bottles should be clearly labeled. You should also take your prescriptions with you.
5. When traveling by air keep the medicine in your carry-on bag rather than in checked luggage.
6. If you get a medication in the country you are visiting, also make sure it is legal in your country of origin should you return with it.

A personal example from Joachim Reimann:

A somewhat related example from my personal history is as follows. While this did not involve a serious medical condition, the example illustrates what can happen when you are in another country. I was born with a deviated septum. In this condition, the thin wall (septum) between your nasal passages is not centered. Therefore one nasal passage is smaller than the other. This can make it difficult to breathe through your nose (especially when you have congestion). To deal with the condition I sometimes use a non-prescription nasal decongestant spray. I was curious if something similar is available in Germany and approached a pharmacy (Apotheke) while traveling there in the 1990s. Some options such as saline solutions existed but they did not seem satisfactory. The pharmacist was, however, very curious about my US product and asked to see it. He then copied down all of the active ingredients from my spray's label. It appeared that, as a regular part of his profession, he mixed some medications in the back of his shop. I don't know if he ever did anything with the ingredients of my medications.

My contact with the German pharmacist was prompted by curiosity rather than an immediate need for the spray. But the interaction highlighted that I was in a completely different environment than I was accustomed to. (A word of caution: some nasal sprays can be habit-forming when over-used, a condition technically called *rhinitis medicamentosa*).[118]

Some of the above examples involve people who are temporarily in a country. They show that even then, dealing with medications you need is complex. For permanent immigrants, the problems are even more substantial. Here are more examples that illustrate the point.

Specific Medication Example: Antibiotics

Antibiotics are medications that treat bacterial infections. They may make it hard for bacteria to grow and multiply or kill bacteria outright. The discovery of this treatment was a major advance in medicine. Suddenly, lethal diseases such as tuberculosis, smallpox, cholera, diphtheria, pneumonia, typhoid fever, and syphilis, among others, could be cured. The average lifespan, particularly in developed countries, increased.[119]

At the same time, using antibiotics is complicated. There are several types of basic drug. Some people are allergic to one type (e.g., penicillin) but can take another without problems. Proper use of antibiotics is essential because doing otherwise can cause more drug-resistant bacteria to develop.[120] As a result, the medications become less effective (or, in some cases, completely ineffective).

Antibiotic use in the world: A 2018 World Health Organization (WHO) report described wide differences in antibiotic use between various countries. People in some countries probably overuse antibiotics while those in other places lack sufficient access to them. Locations where antibiotics are used most frequently include North America, Europe, and the Middle East. By contrast, countries in sub-Saharan Africa and parts of Southeast Asia had some of the lowest consumption rates.[121]

Antibiotic use rates have also changed over time. Worldwide they rose by 46% between 2000 and 2018. This trend was especially pronounced in low- and middle-income countries. In those locations, the rate increased by 76% during the same time period. The largest increases occurred in North Africa and the Middle East region (111%) as well as South Asia (116%). In contrast, antibiotic use in high-income countries tended to remain stable between 2000 and 2018.[122]

Laws around antibiotic use also change from country to country. In Latin America, for example, antibiotics are easily obtained over the counter. In the US they require a prescription from a licensed physician.

Antibiotic use among immigrants: Patterns of antibiotic use among migrants have drawn great attention because, as they travel to a new country, people experience different social norms and environments compared to local populations. Thus, the migrant population might report unique antibiotic use patterns. One study conducted in the US found that, compared with the local population, migrants were 17% more likely to expect antibiotics from a doctor.[123] It has also been reported that Latino immigrants in the United States may use non-prescribed antibiotics more frequently.[124,125] They may be accustomed to getting antibiotics over the counter. If living along the US-Mexico border, they likely go to Mexico to obtain the medication. The literature suggests that many Latinos in the United States also self-prescribe antibiotics because of financial barriers and an inaccurate belief that such medications help treat viral infections.

VACCINES

The COVID-19 pandemic has highlighted the importance of disease prevention through vaccines. Locally approved vaccines can vary from country to country. As we write this, COVID-19 vaccines for Pfizer and Moderna have been approved in the US for some time. Novavax was approved for emergency use on July 13, 2022.[126] A Johnson and Johnson vaccine was originally approved. But now there are cautions about using this vaccine because it was linked to the development of blood clots and severe bleeding in several cases.[127]

Not every country uses US FDA-approved vaccines (exclusively or at all). In Australia, the AstraZeneca vaccine is approved, though limited to people over 50 years of age. China uses Sinovac and Sinopharm. Russia and Hungary use a vaccine called Sputnik V. Russia also uses EpiVacCorona and Covicac. Brazil also uses Sinovac.

Such patterns highlight the complexities immigrants face when they move from country to country. Some vaccines also have properties that complicate disease detection tests in countries where the vaccine is infrequently used or not well-known. As noted in our introduction, the Bacillus Calmette–Guérin (BCG) vaccine is commonly used in a multitude of countries outside the US to prevent tuberculosis. These include Mexico and Central America. But it can also lead to a false-positive reaction to a TB skin test.[128]

The US has not conducted large-scale immunization using BCG because tuberculosis is relatively rare there. Instead, it has relied on detecting and treating latent tuberculosis to control the disease. As such, healthcare systems, employers, and others may not be fully aware of the links between the vaccines and a false positive TB skin test. This can create confusion and lead to unnecessary complications including those impacting employment.

According to the US Department of Labor's Occupational Safety and Health Administration (OSHA), employers, for example, "must make an evaluation and vaccine available to all employees with reasonably anticipated occupational exposure."[129] In addition, it is recommended that people in certain high-risk occupations should have access to a periodic TB skin test. All parties thus need to be fully informed about the possible false positives in some tests, particularly in the case of people who were born and raised in a different country.

Vaccine campaigns: As most of us have seen during the COVID-19 pandemic, some people are very reluctant to get vaccinated. There are many reasons for such "vaccine hesitancy." Social media has perpetuated all kinds of rumors and misinformation about vaccinations. One, for example, makes the physically impossible claim that vaccines can make you magnetic.[130] At the same time, very rare but valid side effects can occur.

The Centers for Disease Control and Prevention (CDC) describes common side effects as fatigue, headache, muscle pain, chills, fever, and nausea.[131] In the past, some groups in the US, especially those from culturally, racially, and linguistically distinct groups were subjected to unethical and harmful medical experiments. These people understandably see medical care involving new prevention and treatment methods with suspicion.[132] One study, for example, showed that vaccine hesitancy in the US population was highest among Black Americans.[133]

It is thus important that vaccine campaigns include trusted community members. One possibility is to engage Community Health Workers (CHWs) also known as *Promotoras*. These are local community leaders with some healthcare knowledge who can reach out to people in local neighborhoods and can connect community members with healthcare providers.[134] In our local city, San Diego, Community *Promotoras* have helped take information about the COVID-19 vaccine directly to Mexican Americans. They have handed out free facemasks and fliers on vaccines in front of grocery stores and to people they know.[135]

The value of such contributions has received increasing international recognition.[136] Starting on July 1, 2022, the US California Department of Health Care Services, for example, added a Community Health Worker benefit to its public healthcare insurance (Medi-Cal) plans.[137] Similar efforts have been underway in other US states such as Minnesota, Oregon, and Indiana. To complicate matters, CHWs' vaccination efforts are handled very differently from country to country.

> **An Example from Dolores:**
> One of our long-time friends who has a professional background in public health recently moved to a small town in the interior of Mexico. There she observed how COVID-19 vaccines were administered.
>
> One day a truck with a loudspeaker on top drove through town and told the residents to all meet at a certain location. The people in the town followed those instructions and were given the vaccine. Then, at a later

date, the truck came back. It was time for the second dose. This was administered in the same way at the same location. It was our friend's impression that everyone in town was vaccinated.

This example does not mean that people in various locations, including immigrants, are immune from absurd rumors that are spread on social media platforms. Some we have heard include the idea that injected vaccines include a tracking device. This would probably worry almost everyone. But it would be of particular concern to undocumented immigrants who fear deportation. This is a myth. Another piece of disinformation is that vaccines are designed to slowly kill specific low-income populations to lessen the financial burdens they create for the broader society. For people who trust and have traditionally relied on the media for accurate information, this can be very scary. Given these types of problems, it is always important to do the research and find trustworthy sources before rejecting a vaccine that may save your life or the life of someone you love.

Dolores' example illustrates how procedures are handled in different countries. Getting vaccinations in the US, even in smaller communities, can be complex. A computer is sometimes needed to set up appointments. In our case, inputting health insurance information while registering for an appointment was required even though the vaccine was free. How does someone who is not computer literate (or even literate at all) negotiate such systems? Maybe we can learn how to do things better from the methods in that small Mexican town.

TRADITIONAL HEALING

Some immigrants come from cultures where various traditional and holistic healing methods are used. Our professional experience has shown that immigrant communities often bring healing traditions with them. Providers in their new countries thus need to be familiar with immigrants' outlook on health and healing. Here are a few examples:

Curanderismo is a traditional healing practice that originated in Latin America (particularly Mexico). A curandero specializes in herbs, waters, spiritual approaches, massages, prayer, and other methods to treat physical, emotional, mental, and presumed spiritual illnesses. Curanderismo tends to mix indigenous and Catholic religious elements.[138] Parts of curanderismo are thought to reflect 16th Century European medicine. While it integrates such elements, curanderismo is not a system that simply throws various practices together. Instead, Renaldo Malduro describes it as entailing a "coherent world view of healing that has deep historical roots."[139]

Ayurvedic medicine (Ayurveda) is an ancient healing art from India that is still practiced today. It uses a holistic approach to physical and mental health. Treatments mainly use herbs but also include substances derived from animals, metals, and minerals. These are combined with traditional diets, yogic exercise, meditation, amulets, and lifestyle improvements.[140]

Traditional Arabic and Islamic Medicine (TAIM) incorporates herbs, spiritual therapies, dietary practices, mind-body practices, and physical manipulation techniques. Depending on the circumstances, these are used individually or together. TAIM incorporates Chinese, Persian, and Ayurvedic practices and is sometimes used in combination with modern medicine to treat infertility and other medical conditions.[141]

Traditional Chinese Medicine (TCM) is another ancient form of treatment that often combines acupuncture, Tai Chi (which uses certain gentle movements, mental focus, breathing, and relaxation), massage, balanced food recommendations, and herbs. It is used to treat pain and a variety of illnesses (e.g. respiratory diseases).[142]

Given that clear research-based evidence addressing these practices is limited, some in Western medical professions are skeptical about the efficacy of these treatments. Overall, available information supports some traditional practices but warns against others. For example, the Latin American tradition of eating *nopales* (prickly pear cactus) to help regulate blood sugar has been supported by research.[143,144] Similar results have been found for *karela* (bitter melon) which is commonly used in Asian cultures. A broad review of the scientific literature points out that traditional South Asian (Indian) medicines have shown effectiveness in controlling type 2 diabetes.[145] Evidence also suggests that acupuncture is helpful in reducing chronic pain.[146]

While such results are positive, the National Center for Complementary and Integrative Health warns that problems with traditional medicine have also been evident. Some Ayurvedic preparations have, for example, been found to contain toxic amounts of lead, mercury, or arsenic. Similarly, research on traditional Chinese medicine has shown that some herbal products include contaminants such as pesticides and metals that can cause illness.[140]

Several of the treatment approaches described above are ancient. For many ill and distressed people, these methods have helped. Therefore, Western medicine can't simply dismiss such treatments as worthless. Since some treatments are useful and others can be potentially dangerous, it is important to carefully investigate traditional methods and learn which work and which do not. Therefore the research and practice communities should explore mechanisms that cause some to be effective, and then include those results in their overall knowledge base. Some professionals have advocated for the coordination of modern and traditional medicine, especially in primary care.[147] A careful scientific exploration of specific traditional healing methods would enhance the viability of that idea.

THINGS THAT INFLUENCE HOW PROVIDERS PRACTICE

In the US, providers are required to use methods that represent the "standard of care" or "standard of practice." The standard of practice for psychologists in California is, for example, defined as the "level of skill, knowledge, and care in diagnosis and treatment ordinarily possessed and exercised by other reasonably careful and prudent psychologists in the same or similar circumstances at the time in question."[148] In plain language, this means that people should get at least adequate treatment, no matter which provider they go to. This does not mean providers have to be the greatest experts in a certain area. They just have to be competent.

Other countries and organizations have also developed medical standards. In 2015 the World Health Organization, for example, published the Global Standards for Quality Healthcare Services for Adolescents.[149] Many of the eight standards it describes focus on what healthcare facilities should do. But, in part, Standard 4 also states that "healthcare providers demonstrate the technical competence required to provide effective health services to adolescents." It then goes on to also note that patient privacy and confidentiality need to be protected. This is an important factor for people who worry that their medical conditions will become public knowledge and damage their reputations.

Immigrants who access their new country's medical system may, at times, be surprised by the number and types of tests that they need to go through. In part, this is driven by the need to check on, and at least rule out, any conditions that may relate to a patient's symptoms. In other words, it's being careful and diligent. But some doctors have also warned that, if taken too far, this practice results in "defensive medicine." The term is used to describe a situation in which providers go beyond a reasonable use of tests, medical procedures, medications, and even hospitalizations to avoid being sued for malpractice. As a consequence healthcare costs increase, and patients can be put under unnecessary strain.[150]

Why would providers be overly concerned about their services and order tests and treatments that are not really called for? Paul Rubin from the *New York Times* notes that the US is the most lawsuit-prone country in the world. People in the US spend roughly $310 billion a year on lawsuits.[151] More specifically Juspoint reports that an estimated 85,000 medical malpractice lawsuits are filed in the US each year.[152] So, it is not surprising that physicians become cautious.

MATERNAL HEALTH

Maternal health is another area that affects immigrants' experiences and expectations. This is a complex topic that could fill its own book. A brief overview follows. We hope it stimulates our readers to learn more.

Pregnancy, childbirth, and raising a small baby can be particularly challenging for immigrants. When women get pregnant shortly before leaving their country of origin or while traveling, they contend with access to medical help which is probably limited and sporadic in many cases. Given the frequent sexual exploitation of migrating women, they may also be faced with pregnancies that have resulted from trauma.

In short, pregnant migrant women can be especially vulnerable to a variety of health risks. They can also face less access to professional care (particularly in the case of undocumented immigrants), and thus a higher risk of complications during pregnancy.[153] The number of pregnant women who die during their migration is not well known. As previously noted, even the overall death rate of migrants is hard to calculate given very limited documentation.[154] Most often, specific incidents come to light through the media with headlines such as "*Woman, Unborn Child Die After Migrants* (are) *Abandoned In A Truck Near* (the) *US-Mexico Border.*"[155]

Severe difficulties with pregnancy while migrating are not universal. The trend varies greatly by immigrant groups. In the US, recent arrivals, particularly those from countries in Central America, South America, South Asia, and sub-Saharan Africa have the most problems.[156]

In addition, the use of medical services among pregnant immigrant women in the US is mixed. On average, they receive less care while pregnant (prenatal care) but more care for pregnancy-related issues once the baby is born (postpartum care).[157] The reason for this trend is not entirely clear. But it may be that immigrants have more difficulties finding care over the course of their pregnancies which then requires more intensive post-delivery interventions. Certainly, increased up-front services that help prevent complications during pregnancy are needed.

Whether, on average, immigrant women have more problems with pregnancy than their native-born counterparts is unclear. The research is not entirely consistent and sometimes appears to reach opposite conclusions. One study, for example, showed that 13% of the immigrants considered for the study actually had fewer cases of infant mortality than the native population. But roughly half of the women in the same study experienced a greater infant mortality rate. The conclusion is that, overall, infant mortality rates are a problem among immigrants. The risk for such mortality is greatest among refugees, non-European migrants to Europe, and foreign-born blacks in the US.[158] Such conditions most directly impact immigrants experiencing low socioeconomic circumstances. At the same time, researchers need to learn more about the 13% that had better-than-average infant survival rates. What actions and attitudes on the part of immigrants contributed to this outcome? One possible reason, especially among people from Latin American countries, is that they have cultural practices that promote health and can reduce infant mortality (see discussions about the "Latino paradox" later in this book).

Despite mixed information, one thing is clear: healthcare systems have to be more culturally attuned to their patients. Succinctly put by Frankie Fair and colleagues, "new models of maternity care are needed which go beyond clinical care and address migrant women's unique socioeconomic and psychosocial needs."[159]

QUESTIONS TO CONSIDER

Given all of the prior discussions, below are a few questions immigrants can ask themselves before migrating to a new country:

1. Do I have, or suspect I have any medical conditions? If so, have they been confirmed by a doctor or other healthcare provider in my country of origin or while I was traveling?

2. Did I get any helpful medications for these conditions (prescribed or not)?

3. Will these medications be available in my new country? If so, will I need to get a prescription?

4. What other helpful treatments, if any, did I have in my country of origin?

5. Will these same treatments be available in my new country?

6. What documents about my health and any medications do I need to take with me when I migrate?

7. Am I traveling with infants or small children? If so, do they have any medical problems?

8. How do I connect with the healthcare system in my new country?

9. Do I have healthcare insurance? What do I need to do to use that insurance or get a different one when I go to a new country?

10. Some countries also screen for preexisting medical conditions before they allow immigrants or even routine travelers to enter.[42] What are the related laws in the country I want to migrate to?

RESOURCES:

- For more information about the US Food and Drug Administration rules and recommendations for bringing foreign medications into the US please visit:

  https://www.fda.gov/consumers/consumer-updates/5-tips -traveling-us-medications

- In part, the European Commission has a somewhat similar role to the US FDA although it is less centralized than the FDA. Specifically, the European Union regulates the approval of medical drugs and devices through a system of agencies in its member states.[160]

- For more information on medication approval in the European Union please see: https://www.ema.europa.eu/en/ about-us/what-we-do/authorisation-medicines

5

CULTURE, IMMIGRATION, AND HEALTH

To understand the connections between immigration, culture, trauma, health, and the spiritual perceptions around wellness, we have to think about a number of different factors. This complex mixture has been shown in some popular movies. One of our favorites illustrating these dynamics is the 2019 romantic comedy "Last Christmas."[161]

We will not give the plot away. But the story revolves around a family from the former Yugoslavia who has immigrated to the UK. There they face the challenges of stress, discrimination, heart disease, and trauma that impact multiple generations. For example, in one of the movie's scenes, a daughter and her mother visit their doctor. Sensing family distress, the doctor suggests that the mother make friends. The mother responds: "...all my friends have been murdered." In another scene, two daughters talk about how "...we are not lucky you and me. We have had to endure the sacrifices of our parents."

In short, serving immigrants requires an understanding of acculturation, how cultural practices impact health, and how well healthcare systems, including individual providers, are able to know and account for immigrants' approaches to illness and well-being. These are the topics for our next discussion.

ACCULTURATION OVERVIEW

When immigrants reach a new country, they adapt to the unfamiliar circumstances they encounter in a variety of ways. This adaptation is often called acculturation. From a healthcare perspective, acculturation has been defined as the "process of learning and incorporating the values, beliefs, language, customs, and mannerisms of the new country immigrants and their families are living in, including behaviors that affect health such as dietary habits, activity levels, and substance use".[162]

Essentially acculturation involves personal and social adaptations that happen when groups of individuals having different cultures come into constant and direct contact. In other words, it's when an immigrant begins to gain and adjust to the norms of their adoptive country. At the most basic level, it is an individual's process of cultural change.[163] But cultural changes do not only happen with immigrants. They can also happen in a country's native culture as it is exposed to and influenced by new cultural groups.

Acculturation involves many aspects of life. These include basic attitudes, language use, political views, economic status, personal values, dietary preferences, types of entertainment people enjoy, and what customs people engage in. But people do not acculturate in only one way. Our first book (*Immigrant Concepts*) in this series goes into detail about how this happens.[164] We will not repeat all of that here. But a brief overview is as follows:

Researchers have identified four basic ways people adapt to a new country.[165] Some choose to discard the language and culture of their home country as they adapt to their new home. This is traditionally called assimilation. Some choose not to adopt the language and traditions of their new country. This may mean their ability to engage in social and routine daily activities is limited to ethnic neighborhoods where most people speak the language of their home countries. Still others choose to learn the language and customs of their adopted country but simultaneously keep those from their country of origin. Consequently, they can function well in different places and with different people. This is often called being bicultural. Finally, some do not fully keep their culture of origin and do not adopt the one from their new country. Rather, they create a new and unique culture.

Acculturation is influenced by many factors. For example, younger people tend to learn a new language faster than their elders. It also impacts how people see their well-being and engage in activities that are likely to be healthy for them. Here are a few examples:

ACCULTURATION AND HEALTH

Some immigrant groups are surprisingly healthy, even when they have undergone difficult journeys and are not financially well off. This is sometimes called the "immigrant paradox." It is thought that new arrivals are healthier because they are more likely to be protected by the cultural norms and traditions they grew up with in their country of origin.

Health researchers have noticed this trend across different parts of the world. In the US they, for example, found that women with Asian and Latin American origins tended to have lower infant mortality rates, higher birth weight, fewer medical diagnoses during delivery, and shorter hospital stays when they were pregnant/delivering than the US-born population.[166] Similar trends have been observed among some immigrant groups in Spain.[167] In addition, female Mexican American immigrants in the US tend to have healthier diets than whites and Mexican American women who were born in the US.[168]

In short, many cases show that immigrants have healthier diets and physical routines than their native-born counterparts. But then, as they become more integrated—certainly in the case of their children—these healthy behaviors erode and become more like those in the adopted society in which they find themselves.[169]

What might account for these trends? As we have previously discussed, exposure to processed and plentiful food that immigrants' bodies are not accustomed to, can cause obesity and with it a multitude of associated illnesses. New immigrants who stick to their traditional diets have a better chance to avoid such problems. In addition, new immigrants may feel as more at risk of catching illnesses in their new environments and may be more inclined to maintain healthy lifestyles.

One of our own studies on tuberculosis prevention supported some of these ideas.[170] We looked at the connections between acculturation, gender, beliefs about health, and people's intent to act on such beliefs among Mexican Americans. To do so we applied the well-established Health Belief Model (HBM) which considers people's perceptions of the following:

1. that a specific disease is serious,
2. that they are at risk of catching it,
3. what barriers to care they believe exist, and other factors.[171]

As we predicted, our study found that less acculturated Mexican Americans saw tuberculosis as a more serious disease and believed they were in greater danger of catching it than their more acculturated counterparts. Because of this, they paid more attention to information on how to prevent tuberculosis. Notably, this group also said that they were likely to encounter more barriers to good care. Across the board, women tended to be more health-conscious than men. Highly acculturated men were least likely to express concern or act on any concern about tuberculosis.

Even with the positive trends noted in the "immigrant paradox," acculturation can be stressful. Learning a new language is a challenge, particularly in later life. In addition, immigrants who differ from many of their native-born counterparts in terms of skin color, clothing, religion, accents, and other features, all too often face discrimination.[172]

Some immigrants also worry about the impact of political circumstances, including changes in those circumstances between their country of origin and their new home. This can influence how the native-born population of their new country see and react to them. Finally, immigrants who had to flee their country of origin often worry about friends and family members they left behind and who may still be in danger.

Acculturation stress has thus been noted as a common problem. This can have a negative impact on health, both in terms of fostering illness and limiting access to care. One study, for example, found connections between such stress and emergency department visits for asthma, insomnia, and general feelings of poor health.[173]

Has the immigrant paradox had an influence on the consequences of COVID-19? Information regarding this question is still limited. The life expectancy of Latino populations decreased over the course of the pandemic. One study looking at these numbers in the context of the immigrant paradox noted that

Latinos have consistently had lower mortality than non-Latino whites. This was still the case. But, on average, the survival rate decreased by two years. This was, however, still one year better than the average survival rate of non-Latino whites.[174] In short, the pandemic had eroded but not completely eliminated positive factors usually described under the term "immigrant paradox."

BECOMING MORE CULTURALLY COMPETENT

All of these examples show that healthcare systems need to become more competent in understanding and treating immigrants. That requires consideration of individual (patient-provider), family, organizational, national, and international factors.

To provide individuals and organizations with guidelines the US Department of Health & Human Services, Office of Minority Health has developed National Standards for Culturally and Linguistically Appropriate Services (CLAS).[175] Many US companies and local governments use these standards to enhance their services and check how effective those efforts are.

In addition, professional agencies have developed cultural competence standards. The US National Association of Social Workers (NASW), for example, cites standards that focus on a practitioner's ethics and values. These include:

1. self-awareness around cultural issues,
2. cross-cultural knowledge and skills,
3. culturally effective approaches to service delivery,
4. activities that empower and advocate for clients as well as those that help build a diverse workforce,

5. fluency in a second language or knowledge on how best to use interpretive services including with those who have hearing impairments, and

6. displaying leadership in advancing cultural competence in their workplace and communities.[176]

The complete standards can be found online at: https://www.soc ialworkers.org/Practice/NASW-Practice-Standards-Guide lines/Standards-and-Indicators-for-Cultural-Competence-in-Social-Work-Practice

Other US organizations offering guidance on cultural competence in healthcare include the American Hospital Association (AHA),[177] the American Medical Association (AMA),[178] and the Centers for Disease Control and Prevention (CDC).[179]

Academics have come up with a number of models that reflect the attitudes and behaviors we need to consider to fully understand cultural competence. On a fundamental level, it can be said that culture reflects a pattern of social norms, behaviors, institutions, and beliefs that is specific to a group of people. Individuality is how all of us are different. Universal traits reflect those that are common to all known human cultures worldwide. This is sometimes referred to as the anthropological universal. In other words, it is how all people are alike (e.g., that all humans use some form of language, that we listen to music, that we create art). Culture, as discussed in this book, is how some of us are alike. In other words, some of us share specific values and practices. In this process, we keep in mind that not all people from a certain cultural background adhere to the norms that are generally ascribed to their group. In fact, people from a certain group or nationality are often quite diverse. We will later address what that means when providers and other caregivers interact with their patients.

Some models of cultural competence are quite complex. The Purnell Model, for example, considers how global society, communities, families, and the individual all influence pregnancy, nutrition, high-risk behaviors such as drug and tobacco use, spirituality, healthcare practices, and many other aspects of our lives. It also describes stages and types of cultural incompetence and competence.[180] The model, presented here with Dr. Purnell's permission, is as follows:

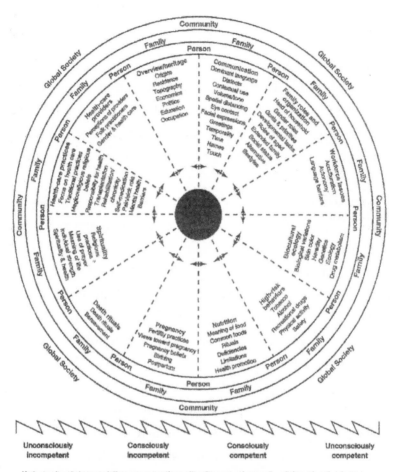

Variant cultural characteristics: age, generation, nationality, race, color, gender, religion, educational status, socioeconomic status, occupation, military status, political beliefs, urban versus rural residence, enclave identity, marital status, parental status, physical characteristics, sexual orientation, gender issues, and reason for migration (sojourner, immigrant, undocumented status).

Unconsciously incompetent: not being aware that one is lacking knowledge about another culture
Consciously incompetent: being aware that one is lacking knowledge about another culture
Consciously competent: learning about the client's culture, verifying generalizations about the client's culture, and providing culturally specific interventions
Unconsciously competent: automatically providing culturally congruent care to clients of diverse cultures

The Purnell Model for Cultural Competence. Printed with permission from LD Purnell.

Other models focus more directly on healthcare provision. The many ways of looking at cultural competence all have their uses.[181] For this book, we focus on direct interactions between providers and patients, what steps organizations can take to further competent actions and global issues that impact healthcare.

Individual Level

How do individual healthcare providers become more culturally competent? Our research provided some answers. It investigated what attitudes and circumstances facilitated culturally competent actions among physicians who treated Mexican Americans.

Of the factors we considered, only (1) recognizing the importance of a patient's culture in healthcare and (2) understanding the potential for biased views were directly linked to a doctor's cultural competence. In addition, the practical education doctors receive is important. Simply seeing Mexican Americans in clinical practice did not guarantee effectiveness with this cultural group. But having a more formal supervised internship or experience in a community clinic where providers receive support and supervision while they work with culturally and linguistically distinct populations was helpful.[182] The research developed a model which is presented here. It is not purely theoretical but was verified through statistical analyses. While our research looked at only one particular cultural group and disease, we believe it is also applicable to many different situations.

What Predicts Culturally Competent Actions?

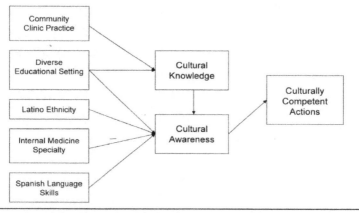

Reimann JO, Talavera GA, Salmon M, Nuñez J, Velasquez RJ. (2004) Cultural competence among physicians treating Mexican Americans who have diabetes. A structural model. *Social Science & Medicine*. 2004; 59, 2195-2205

Here are a few more considerations for healthcare providers' work with culturally different patients.

Using Authority in Constructive Ways: Doctors are seen as influential authorities in most societies. This includes a variety of culturally and linguistically distinct groups. Such a platform gives physicians the opportunity to direct patients toward certain treatments and diagnostic procedures. But they can also provide health education that engages the patient as a full partner in services. For example, a study Joachim worked on looked at patients coming to a community clinic located in sight of the US-Mexico border. It asked these patients what had prompted them to get some type of colorectal cancer screening. The most influential prompts were that their doctor had discussed such screening with them and that they now had more knowledge about cancer. Worries about generally feeling in poor health and having insurance also contributed to their decision.[183]

Language & Interpretive Services: It is important for providers to know details about interpreters. Are they professionals or family members? Do the professional interpreters know the regional dialects of the people we work with? Professional interpreters use two primary approaches. Some try to keep their own personalities out of the process as much as possible. Others also serve as cultural brokers. The latter clarifies the specific meanings and context of what a patient is saying if the provider is unfamiliar with such contexts. This can be particularly important in emergency situations where immediately clear information is essential.[184]

Example from Joachim Reimann

Over much of his career my father, Dr. Bernhard Reimann, worked at a US Army hospital. The facility was located adjacent to a military base that helped train elements of the German armed forces. As a German immigrant my father, of course, understood these soldiers' language. One late evening he received an emergency call from the facility. A German soldier had been transported to the hospital and appeared desperate to tell the staff something important. No other German speaker was available, so my father drove to the hospital in record time. Upon his arrival, he asked the soldier what he was trying to say. The reply was *"Ich muss schiffen."* This is a colloquial expression that translates into "I really have to pee."

Everyone had a good laugh, including the soldier (once he was able to use the bathroom). But the situation could well have been worse if the patient had something more critical to say and the available interpreter did not know colloquialisms. (The literal translation of the solder's expression is "I have to ship.") I do not know why the soldier went to the hospital. Presumably, he had a significant medical condition that required prompt treatment. As I understand it, my father was able to provide further translations that helped in the process of diagnosis and treatment.

The CLAS Standards recognize that sometimes when an interpreter is needed, adult relatives are the most or only viable option. However, the CLAS Standards also specifically note that using children or adolescents in the role of the interpreter is never a good idea. Obviously, children do not need to know the intimate details of their relatives' health status. This is likely to be embarrassing for them as well as the family's adults. Children are also not emotionally and intellectually mature enough to handle interpretive responsibilities.

Dietary Practices: It comes as no surprise that what we eat has a significant influence on our health. But, as we have previously noted, specific diets vary from culture to culture. In many countries, food and supplements are an important part of traditional healing. To maximize treatment effectiveness, it is important that healthcare providers know all of the substances, including homeopathic ones, that a patient is taking.

How Problems are Described: Some symptoms can have either physical or psychological causes (or both). People who have a panic attack, for example, tend to experience increased heart rates, chest pains, dizziness, sweating, and problems breathing that can feel like a heart attack.

When a patient has such symptoms, it is important to consider physical causes first. But doctors also need to know that, in some cultures, it is considered more appropriate to acknowledge physical rather than emotional problems.[185]

Emotional disturbances may be seen as personal weaknesses and thus shameful, both by the person experiencing them (self-stigma) and by others (public stigma). Assumptions that an individual's emotional problems imply personal deficits can also reflect badly on the person's entire family. Thus acknowledging psychological problems and talking about them is avoided.[186] We suspect that there are few people who like to acknowledge mental health problems. But cultural taboos against such admissions are particularly strong in some traditional Asian, Latin American, and African societies.[187,188,189]

In some cases, emotional distress is just seen as a regular part of life as opposed to a known and treatable condition. So it makes sense that healthcare providers who first see patients are knowledgeable about cultural attitudes, explore symptoms in the context of mental health, and make referrals to a specialist when appropriate. In our clinical experience with culturally and linguistically distinct groups, immigrants often present themselves as having headaches and other physical symptoms. But they are usually able to acknowledge psychological symptoms if asked about them in safe and confidential environments.

Consider Body Language and Speech: Many social practices vary across cultures. Steady eye contact is, for example, seen as showing interest, honesty, and engagement in the US. In contrast, direct eye contact is seen as a sign of aggression and disrespect in some Asian countries like Japan, South Korea, and China.[190] Given these very different reactions, mistakes are likely if providers are unaware of cultural nuances.

Gestures also have different meanings across cultures. Curling up the index finger usually means "come closer" in the US and Europe. But in many Asian countries it is considered rude and something you only do with dogs. We understand that making such a gesture in the Philippines is so unacceptable it can get people arrested.

Providers should also be aware of cultural differences in how loudly people speak, how animated they are in conversations, and how close they come to another person. What is seen as an aggressive and rude invasion of personal space may be perfectly normal in another culture.

Example by Joachim Reimann

While it is good to be aware of cultural traditions it is also important to understand that much diversity exists within each culture. This is based on individual differences, acculturation, and a host of other factors. In my practice, I have learned that Muslim women, particularly those from the Middle East, generally do not shake hands with someone from a different gender. Physical contact is seen as too familiar. Rather, they put their hand across their chest and smile politely. Therefore I do not put my hand out in greeting or farewell. But there have been occasions when a woman, even in traditional Muslim garb, sticks her hand out and leaves it there until I take it, even if I have hesitated to do so. It may well be a sign of respect that says, "I'm acculturating and respect your traditions." I still don't reach my hand out in the case of Muslim women. But I'm not surprised if they reach out to me and adjust to their actions.

Family Dynamics: Family roles tend to change with immigration and acculturation. Children, who generally learn a new language more quickly than adults, may be called upon by family members to interpret for them. As previously noted, this responsibility puts a burden on adolescents for which they are not developmentally ready. In a healthcare setting, it is likely inappropriate to learn about a parent's or other relatives' medical history and current concerns. A family may come into a healthcare setting expecting their minor child to translate for them. This is probably the way the family does things in other places like the grocery store. But in healthcare, it is best if the facility either has a provider who speaks the family's language or uses professional interpretive services. US forensic medical settings, where evaluations and other records will play a role in court, often require that the interpreter be formally trained as a Certified Medical Interpreter. For more information on this topic please see https://www.ncihc.org/certification

Socioeconomic Status: Similarly to family dynamics, socioeconomic status can change for the worse with migration. Suddenly a doctor, attorney, or other professional is doing unskilled labor. That can take some adjustment and likely impacts financial access to healthcare.

Gender: Finding a provider who matches a patient's gender is often important (for example if the patient is asked to disrobe). While this is likely true regardless of culture, it may involve special religious or social taboos in some circumstances. It is particularly notable that women who have undergone forced migration have all too often been raped or otherwise sexually exploited in their home country or on their journey to a new place. Being asked to disrobe in front of a stranger or having to tell him about physical issues can be especially difficult for women with this kind of trauma history.

Recognizing and Respecting Individual Differences: Healthcare workers and providers are certainly encouraged to learn about the norms various cultures tend to espouse. But the common medical admonition that "the patient is a case of one" (in other words, is an individual) still applies. If providers use their understanding of cultural norms as background information but also remember that individuals within any group are very diverse, they can be most effective. Otherwise, they run the risk of developing yet another stereotype.

Letting People Know About Services: How do providers let people know about available services? What methods work best when we attempt to inform a community through outreach and education? Letting people know that treatment is safe and confidential is important in matching people with healthcare providers. Providers in individual or small private practices will probably have to engage in some outreach. Having staff members who speak the community's language is important. Larger organizations will have additional challenges. These will be discussed in our next section.

Organizational Level:

Culturally effective healthcare services do not only depend on individual providers. Organizations, clinics, and hospitals also need to offer a supportive environment in which such services can flourish. Some of the questions organizational administrators can ask themselves include:

1. Do I have professional training services that teach and mentor my providers and support staff? It is particularly important to note that support staff members play an essential role in creating a welcoming environment. They are often the first ones to encounter patients and thus set the tone for an organization. The comfortable patient is more likely to have productive interactions with their providers. Conversely, "poor treatment by receptionist"

was listed as one of nine main problems restricting access to care in one of our studies.[191]

2. Do I have access to professional interpreters that cover the languages (including regional dialects) my organization needs to serve our community?

3. Does my organization know the specific language a community speaks?

An example from Joachim Reimann

Some years ago, I was working with an elderly Somali patient. He had received written materials in English about a change in his insurance benefits which made no sense to him (or to me). With his permission, I contacted the responsible entity to address the problem. I explained the situation and a conference call was scheduled. To keep my patient, who would be on the call, fully engaged I requested interpretive services. (We were able to talk well together in treatment. But he was not able to understand more complex and technical conversations.) Prior to the call, the person arranging the meeting proudly told me that, after much searching, he had been able to enlist the services of a *Samoan* interpreter. Ultimately, we were able to solve the problem. But it illustrates how things can go wrong.

---

4. Does my organization have written materials in various languages available? Do I know the literacy levels often found in the communities I serve? Our own work with the local Somali refugee community, for example, shows that many people we see are not literate. In addition, the Somali language comes from an oral tradition in which

the spelling of some words is not fully developed. Consequently, written information is of little use to some people in this community.

5. Are my staff recruitment and retention policies effective in creating a skilled workforce that reflects the community it serves?

6. Are my providers willing and able to coordinate care with traditional healers when appropriate?

7. Does my organization have viable methods to check treatment outcomes and patient satisfaction so any problems can be identified, and improvements can be made?[192]

In addition, some healthcare organizations have developed culturally attuned programs that help people manage chronic illnesses. One example is nurse-managed diabetes care programs in which patients attend educational activities and learn to care for themselves. Their health continues to be monitored on a regular basis. But they also become more independent.[107,193] It is important to address emotional as well as physical well-being in such programs.[108]

International Level

The countries and regions in our world are increasingly connected through commerce (including multinational corporations), political alliances, and many other factors. This has emphasized a need for what has been described as global competence.[194]

At its core, global competence is made up of certain values, attitudes, actions, and skills.[195] In practical terms that includes proficiency in two or more languages, awareness of differences between cultures, understanding of diverse perspectives, and the ability to work professionally in intercultural and international situations. We would add that such competence also requires an understanding that there is much diversity within cultures. As previously noted, the degree to which people from a specific community adhere to the average "cultural norms" of that group varies greatly.

Given these trends, doctors and other healthcare professionals have increasingly emphasized the importance of competence in global health. This means understanding health across all countries, populations that migrate, displacement due to climate change, worldwide economic relationships that facilitate travel and thus potential disease transmission, how to monitor such transmission so emerging diseases can be dealt with early in their development, and other factors. Global competence in healthcare will require many disciplines so doctors and other healthcare workers can understand and work with each other toward a common goal of better services and support. This requires cooperation and coordination between epidemiological, cultural, financial, environmental, ethnic, political, public health, and legal arenas. Specific fields such as medical anthropology, psychology, sociology, medicine, biostatistics, and others can all make significant contributions.[196,197] Such coordination can potentially recognize and effectively negotiate the fact that we live in an interconnected world in which health and wellness are global rather than country-by-country issues.[198]

DIRECTIONS FORWARD

While researchers and clinicians have learned some things about culturally competent care, healthcare professionals need to understand much more about this topic. How do we increase our knowledge about ways to make service approaches more culturally effective on an international level?

Needs Assessments: One way is to think about our methods for conducting research. By tradition, health research uses an approach that generates data (numbers). We can then plug those into formal statistical analyses. But this method requires us to know the right questions upfront. What happens in the case of populations for which little research exists? Here are some ideas:

Over our career, we have advocated for needs assessments that consider various types of information. These include community and faith-based newspapers, culturally focused websites, and interviews with people who work with specific populations.[199] Many traditional academics have not included these sources because they have not been scientifically (peer) reviewed and accepted. Such sources can, in fact, have biased agendas. But in our experience, they have also brought insights into legitimate community attitudes, needs, concerns, and perceptions when we consider them in an open but careful way.

When doing the actual needs assessment we have used what is sometimes called a mixed methods approach.[200] First, we gain knowledge about a community through structured but open-ended conversations with its members. Then this information identifies specific questions later studies using quantitative methods (for example questionnaires that can be statistically analyzed) need to ask.[199]

Needs assessments are designed to bring changes that enhance healthcare services to various communities. During one of our projects, we envisioned the steps that can lead to such change.[191] The graphic is as follows:

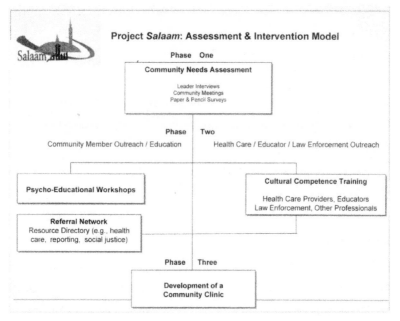

Results from the needs assessment lead to "phase two." This is designed to educate the community about healthcare services and provide them with a referral network of providers who are known to understand their specific culture and common immigration experiences. It also trains healthcare providers, educators, law enforcement personnel, and others who come in frequent contact with a community about culturally competent approaches.

A potential "phase 3" involves starting a community clinic that has particular expertise in an immigrant population. There are potential risks and benefits to this idea. One risk is that other healthcare systems may decide a specific population will be exclusively served by the specialized clinic. This complacency can result in decreased efforts to understand and become competent in working with the community. But such a clinic can also serve as a best practices model that others emulate. Here is one example.

Combining Research and Treatment: One of the facilities we believe serves as a good health service approach is the Access Community Health & Research Center in Dearborn Michigan USA.[201] The Center combines community-based treatment with research and has particular expertise in serving Arab Americans. It partners with universities for the research component. In addition, it integrates mental, general, dental, environmental, and public health into one cohesive system. Researchers then test the system in various ways, and the center uses research outcomes to improve its services. This is not a one-time event but an ongoing process that continually refines the organization's effectiveness.

International Cooperation

The COVID-19 pandemic has clearly shown us that the world needs a better way to understand, track, and intervene in emerging contagious diseases. History has also taught us that COVID-19 will not be the last pandemic. In July of 2022 the World Health Organization, for example, declared that the spread of a viral disease called monkeypox (Mpox) was a global public health emergency.[202] To date, Mpox is not known to be as deadly or easily spread as COVID-19. But its spread does alert us to the ongoing and increasing need for international coordination and allocation of healthcare resources. Toward the end of 2022, the World Health Organization also noted that influenza has spread among multiple countries, particularly in the Earth's Northern Hemisphere. This, again, highlights the ongoing need for global cooperation around health and illness.

One concern is whether or not countries have the staffing capacity and infrastructure to prevent and treat emerging illnesses. An adequate supply of healthcare workers is one major element in that process. A shortfall in healthcare workers in certain countries is nothing new. Nursing shortages, for example, contributed to the development of the US Exchange Visitor Program which essentially imported nurses from the Philippines starting in the 1960s.[203] The program is not limited to nursing and continues as we write this book. Aside from nurses, Exchange Visitor Visas are available for physicians, professors, research scholars, students, trainees, interns, and people in other classifications.

While such initiatives are helpful, the process of having healthcare credentials accepted internationally is still far from easy. Sometimes it is even difficult to move across state lines in a single country. We, for example, know that it would be easier to transfer our US California psychology license to New Zealand than it would be to transfer it to many other states within the US. This is an obvious and bizarre problem. Such barriers are not limited to the US. But some countries also make specific efforts to recruit healthcare workers across the globe.

> ### Example from Dolores Rodríguez-Reimann
>
> Recently our contacts in Tijuana, Mexico told us that they had encountered German companies who were recruiting healthcare workers there. We were curious and followed up on the report. Sure enough, the information we found showed that healthcare facilities such as Berlin's Charité University Hospital (Charité – Universitätsmedizin Berlin, one of Europe's largest and most prestigious facilities), had recruited Mexican nurses and caregivers who were now working in German facilities.[204]

These efforts have been prompted by a long-term, substantial, and ongoing nursing shortage in Germany. Efforts have been in progress to make the acceptance of foreign-trained nurses easier.[205] But problems continue. For example, Thomas Krakau, the head of nursing at a hospital group has been quoted as saying that a country-wide system for accepting foreign credentials needs to be developed. He further expressed the concern that German states have their individual procedures which make hiring foreign workers difficult and wastes administrative resources.

Fortunately, the COVID-19 pandemic has shown us that traditional barriers limiting foreign-licensed healthcare workers from practicing their profession in a new country can be overcome. Prompted by the pandemic, many jurisdictions softened the restrictions on foreign-trained and foreign-born health workers in high-income countries to better cope with the crisis. Some reports said that healthcare workers had even been flown to hard-hit countries from overseas (e.g., Chinese, Cuban, and Albanian doctors were sent to Italy). Refugee doctors without local licenses were called up in Germany. Some had their immigration fast-tracked in the United Kingdom. In the United States, New York City allowed foreign-trained doctors to work. We have seen nothing that shows these providers are less competent than their local counterparts. If anything, UPI has reported that, in the US., foreign-trained doctors are sued less frequently than those who have received their degrees from US medical schools.[206]

It's clear that governments need to increase the worldwide availability of healthcare professionals through mutual training agreements between nations. This would allow universities to teach providers the specific needs and circumstances of more than one country. One such model is presented by the Global Skills Partnership.[207] This approach addresses a wide variety of occupations including healthcare. It allows for the distribution of a labor force where it is most needed. Countries join to provide integrated technology and financing. In December 2018, 163 states adopted the Global Compact for Migration. Global Skill Partnerships are the only specific policy idea included in this agreement. Overall the partnership entails 6 primary dimensions. These are:

1. It addresses future migration pressures (e.g., integration of foreign professionals into host countries). Such migration pressures would likely include those resulting from pandemics and other challenges to healthcare systems. Plans can also identify ways to lessen any resulting drain of skilled personnel in the countries of origin.

2. It involves employers in host and home countries who identify and train for specific skills. This improves the overall learning curve of healthcare workers and speeds up their access to populations who are most in need.

3. It can form public-private partnerships to effectively train people for semi-skilled occupations (e.g., caregivers) that don't require university degrees.

4. It can create or improve worker skill sets before people migrate.

5. It can integrate training for migrants with training for non-migrants in the home country. While that process

addresses differing needs, it can also foster broader learning among both groups.
6. It can improve flexibility so that, ideally, skills are adapted
to specific home and host-country needs.

These efforts represent the beginning of an ongoing process.
To be successful, they will require governments and professional
organizations to reconsider long-held ideas, policies, and laws.
As bad as healthcare emergencies are, they do bring the weaknesses in current healthcare systems and regulations to light
indicating a call for change and thus potential improvements.

Certainly, healthcare professionals need to meet academic
and clinical standards to ensure patient health and safety. But
we can no longer assume that, just because providers received
degrees in a foreign country, they are inadequately trained and
qualified. Their skills can be tested but should not be automatically dismissed. If competent, their international experience,
including language skills, can enhance the ability of immigrant
communities to receive first-class care.

In addition, information on emerging infectious diseases
needs to be shared across countries in real time. This helps ease
human suffering across the globe.

Community education by responsible use of traditional and
social media outlets is one powerful tool in limiting the impact
of pandemics.[208] Distributing accurate information about diseases and ways to prevent them has the potential to change
behaviors to those that foster health.[209] This will, however,
require public education on which media outlets are
trustworthy.

EPILOGUE

As we have said throughout our books in this series, our goal is to provide and explain information that is not widely distributed beyond the world of academic research and theory.

As we have also pointed out, immigrants who are from developing or war-torn countries are more susceptible to certain illnesses and medical conditions. At the same time, they often bring healthy habits with them that serve them well in their new environments. Overall, researchers from the Center for Humanitarian Health at Johns Hopkins School of Public Health conclude that migrants commonly contribute more to their adopted country than they cost.[65] This has been most recently highlighted by their work on the front lines of the COVID-19 pandemic.

Rather than worrying that immigrants bring diseases with them, we can thus acknowledge the benefits they provide. On this topic, Dr. Paul Spiegel from Johns Hopkins University has been quoted as saying "It's not migrants or migration itself that is spreading disease. It may be the situations that they are in and the lack of access to basic care that may exacerbate the situation."

In this book, we do identify healthcare needs and problems that can affect some immigrant groups. But perhaps more importantly, we seek to provide solutions that maximize the contributions immigrants can make while reducing any distress they face.

Our own family and personal histories illustrate the frequent connections between healthcare services and immigration that can span generations. Joachim's father, an immigrant from Germany, was a biologist with medical training who spent over twenty years working at a US hospital. There he was one of the first persons who applied tests using an electron microscope to help diagnose patients. Over time this practice has become established.[210] Upon retirement, Joachim's father created a biology-based clean water system that helped reduce the chance of illness in a small rural community. He was also instrumental in bringing an enhanced 911 emergency number to his community. Joachim's mother was a medical technologist.

One of Dolores' grandfathers learned many healing traditions in Mexico and used them to help others once he migrated to the US. Dolores' mother worked in a nursing home for over ten years. Their examples inspired us to become psychologists and public health researchers.

We suspect that such traditions are far from unique. Variations of our story are repeated in many immigrant families. Nor are they limited to the healthcare arena.

Many traditions, including those in healthcare, are highly entrenched. Changing them is likely to be difficult and will require persistent advocacy. But individuals, healthcare systems, community-based service organizations, and international non-governmental organizations (NGOs) can help. NGOs for example have a history of advocating for a number of social issues. This includes the chance to use various social media outlets and other technologies to inform people.[211] Some of these have specifically focused on health.[212] We hope these efforts continue. We also hope that our books point out some of the things we can do to better understand immigrants' health needs and change services for the better.

GLOSSARY

Acculturation is generally defined as cultural modification and adaptation of an individual, group, or people by learning and integrating traits and norms from another culture. Acculturation is not a one size fits all concept in that it can take many forms.

Acculturation Stress refers to the psychological challenges involved in adapting to a new culture. This stress can be significant especially when acculturation involves major life changes like learning a new language, reduced socioeconomic status, facing discrimination in a new country, etc. Acculturation stress has been acknowledged as an area of clinical concern in the International Classification of Diseases, Tenth Revision, (ICD-10) and the Diagnostic and Statistical Manual of Mental Disorders, Fifth Edition (DSM–5).

In addition, acculturation stress can have a negative impact on physical health and wellbeing and has been connected with emergency department visits for such problems as asthma, insomnia, and general feelings of poor health.

Anogenital Injuries (AGI) is an injury to male or female sex organs, sometimes due to rape and other sexual violence. Most, but not all such injuries are outside the body. Some require surgery.

Antibiotics are medications that treat bacterial infections. They may make it hard for bacteria to grow and multiply, and they can kill bacteria outright. There are several groups of antibiotics. This is important to know since some people are allergic to a specific antibiotic (e.g., penicillin) but can take another type without problems. The most common antibiotics are amoxicillin and amoxicillin/clavulanic acid. The World Health Organization considers them the first or second-line treatment. Broad-spectrum antibiotics (another classification of the medication family) are useful in treating a variety of bacterial infections. But these can also raise the chance that drug-resistant bacteria will develop. Finally, there is a "reserve" group of antibiotics designed to treat specific infections where drug resistant bacteria have caused more commonly used medications to become ineffective. Antibiotics do not treat viral infections (although doctors may give you an antibiotic if you have a viral infection because they do not want a secondary bacterial infection to develop). Proper use of antibiotics is essential because doing otherwise can cause more drug resistant bacteria to develop. That would rob us of an important tool in fighting major and sometimes life-threatening diseases such as tuberculosis. It is particularly important that patients take all of the antibiotics their doctor has prescribed, even after they start to feel better.

Autoimmune Disorders are those in which the body's immune system essentially destroys healthy body tissue by mistake. Examples include rheumatoid and other forms of arthritis, and multiple sclerosis.

Ayurveda is a healing art from India. It uses a holistic approach that incorporates herbs, substances derived from animals, metals, and minerals. These are combined with traditional diets, yogic exercise, meditation, amulets, and lifestyle improvements.

Corona Virus Disease (COVID-19) is an infectious disease caused by the SARS-CoV-2 virus. It is known to particularly impair the lungs but can cause damage to other parts of the body as well. The virus can spread from an infected person's mouth or nose in small liquid particles through coughing, sneezing, speaking, singing or breathing.

Most COVID-19 infections result in mid-to-moderate symptoms. But some people will get seriously ill, require hospitalization, and may even die. Older people and those with conditions such as cardiovascular disease, diabetes, chronic respiratory disease, or cancer are most at risk of serious illness. But anyone can get sick with COVID-19 and even die regardless of age or medical history.

Cultural Competence: The US Office of Minority Health defines "cultural competence" as "having the capacity to function effectively as an individual and an organization within the context of cultural beliefs, behaviors, and needs presented by consumers and their communities." Internationally, cultural competence research and advocacy also emphasizes global health. As such it strives to understand the interconnections between regions, cultural groups, climate change, ecosystems, and political realities as they impact health and wellness.

Curanderismo is a traditional healing practice that originated in Latin America (particularly Mexico). A curandero specializes in herbs, waters, and spiritual approaches, massages, prayer, and other methods to treat physical, emotional, mental, and presumed spiritual illnesses. Curanderismo tends to mix native and Catholic religious elements. Portions of this practice are thought to reflect 16th Century European medicine.

Food Insecurity refers to the limited or uncertain availability of adequate and safe foods. A lack of adequate food can lead to a number of serious medical, psychological, and developmental conditions.[213] For more in food insecurity see: https://www.healthaffairs.org/doi/epdf/10.1377/hlthaff.2015.1257

Global Competence refers to a combination of knowledge, skills, and other capacities that allows people to successfully navigate intercultural and international challenges.

People who are globally and culturally competent are proficient in at least two languages, are aware of the differences and similarities that exist between cultures, understand the diversity that exists within cultures, understands diverse perspectives, and can function at a professional level in intercultural and international situations. For more information on global competence please see: https://www.girlbossmath.com/uploads/1/1/7/5/117585876/nea_global_imperative.pdf

Global Health is a discipline that incorporates aspects of public health, tropical medicine, and many other disciplines. Its primary goal is to improve and gain equal access to health for all of our planet's people by addressing global health issues and solutions through the worldwide collaboration of people, organizations, and governments.

Global Warming refers to increases in the Earth's surface temperatures over time. It has been linked to both "natural" events (such as volcano eruption) as well human activities. Causes related to our human population include commercial deforestation, motor vehicle emissions (carbon dioxide and other toxins), chlorofluorocarbons, overall industrial development, agricultural practices that create carbon dioxide and methane gas, and general overpopulation.

The Health Belief Model (HBM) is a social/psychological construct that seeks to explain and predict health-related actions. The HBM suggests that people's beliefs about health problems, perceived benefits of action, barriers to such action, and self-efficacy explain why they will or will not engage in healthy behaviors. Our research has found that the various parts of the HBM are all important. But how they connect and interact with each other can vary from culture to culture.

Industrial Injuries are those that are caused by an accident at work or that are related to the type of work someone does. They can be physical, psychological or a combination of both. For example, a worker who was the victim of a violent crime may suffer both a physical injury as well as psychological trauma. In some cases an industrial injury can also exacerbate a medical problem that the injured worker had before suffering a work accident or stressor.

Migrations: The Cambridge Dictionary defines migrations as being "the process of people traveling to a new place to live, usually in large numbers."

Mind-Body Dualism takes the position that mental phenomena are not physical or that the mind and body are distinct and separate. It has been discussed by many philosophers but is especially connected to René Descartes.

Pain entails physical suffering, usually caused by illness or injury. There are several known types of pain. Nociceptive pain involves tissue damage from bruising, burns, or other injuries. Neuropathic pain is caused by problems with the human nervous system due to an injury or illness (e.g., irritable bowel syndrome, fibromyalgia, and chronic headaches). Pain can also be thought of as acute or chronic. It becomes chronic when it lasts three or more months. In some instances pain alerts us to existing physical injuries. That can prompt us to deal with the underlying cause. But in some instances, especially when chronic, it does not contribute any practical benefit to our survival. Pain can lead to psychological difficulties. Understandably, chronic and unresolved pain can lead to anxiety, frustration, and depression.

A Pandemic involves the worldwide spread of a new disease. At present viral diseases are most likely to cause a pandemic. In contrast, an epidemic is defines as involving a health condition of concern that develops in a community or region but does not spread any further.

A Promotora (aka Community Health Worker or CHW) is usually a self-taught Latina community member and leader who provides health advice in the neighborhood. This has been a common tradition for some time. Many professional researchers and providers now seek out promotoras because they have the ear of their community. They often train these individuals in public health and employ them as liaisons to spread needed information about prevention, treatment, and related services. The basic concept of a Community Health Worker is not limited to Latinos. We (Dolores and Joachim) have used a similar approach with Middle Eastern and East African populations. We thus believe that this basic approach can be effective across multiple different communities and populations.

Public Health is generally defined as a field of study and practice that seeks to improve the health of individuals and communities. This includes disease prevention and health promotion. In academia, public health is an interdisciplinary area that includes researchers from a variety of relevant areas (e.g. epidemiology, environmental health, the social sciences, community health). Public health research makes efforts to define the impact of certain problems (e.g., environmental tobacco smoke) and identify evidence-based ways in which people can improve their wellness. In practice, public health workers use approaches that will help people and societies change their behavior and become healthier. Examples are sharing vaccine information and anti-smoking campaigns.

Socioeconomic Status refers to the social standing of an individual or group. It tends to consider education, income, and the social status of a person's occupation. The socioeconomic status can undergo a radical change when people immigrate. For example, medical doctors, attorneys and other professionals educated and licensed in their country of origin may not have those credentials accepted in their new home.

Stunting The World Health Organization defines stunting as "impaired growth and development that children experience from poor nutrition, repeated infection, and inadequate psychosocial stimulation. This is an unfortunately common problem in populations who have been exposed to war and other extreme stressors.

Tobacco Use involves many different products. These include cigarettes, cigars, chewing tobacco (dip, snuff), dissolvable tobacco, shisha (which combines tobacco and fruit or vegetable products that are smoked using a hookah), and pipe tobacco. Using tobacco products has been linked to a multitude of illnesses and health conditions. These include lung, laryngeal, esophageal cancer, chronic obstructive pulmonary disease (COPD), chronic bronchitis, and emphysema to name a few. Some tobacco products or related smoking devices (e.g., vaping) have been claimed to be medically safe. But research shows that such claims are not accurate.

Traditional Arabic and Islamic Medicine (TAIM) uses herbs, spiritual therapies, dietary practices, mind-body practices, and physical manipulation techniques. TAIM incorporates Chinese, Persian, and Ayurvedic (Indian) practices and is sometimes used in combination with modern medicine to treat infertility and other medical conditions.

Traditional Chinese Medicine (TCM) often combines acupuncture, Tai Chi, massage, balanced food recommendations, and herbs. It is used to treat pain and a variety of illnesses.

Trauma can include physical injuries, psychological distress, or some combination of both. Physical trauma refers to a clinically serious injury to the body. Most often this is divided into "blunt force trauma" when something strikes but does not necessarily penetrate the body. This can cause concussions, broken bones, and similar injuries. "Penetrating trauma" refers to circumstances in which some object has pierced the body's skin, usually resulting in an open wound. Psychological trauma refers to cognitive and emotional disturbances that can arise from one or more distressing events (e.g., war, domestic violence, auto, and industrial accidents, sexual abuse, and exploitation). Directly experiencing or even witnessing such events often causes overwhelming stress that a person cannot cope with. In many incidents, physical and psychological trauma happens together. Also, some people experience "cumulative trauma" which involves not one but a protracted set of harmful events. In addition "generational trauma" (also sometimes called intergenerational trauma) involves the generational transmission of the oppressive or traumatic effects of a past event. For more on generational trauma please see: https://michaelgquirke.com/recognize-these-intergenerational-trauma-signs-symptoms/

Tuberculosis (TB) is a contagious bacterial infection that usually attacks your lungs. But it can also spread to your brain, spine, and other parts of your body. The bacteria involved is *Mycobacterium tuberculosis*. Most TB can be cured with antibiotics. But there is a concern that the overuse of such medications results in multidrug resistant TB which makes treatment much more difficult. When someone is infected with *Mycobacterium tuberculosis* but does not have active TB the condition is called latent tuberculosis (LTB).

Type 2 Diabetes is a chronic illness that has to do with the way your body produces or uses insulin. Insulin is a hormone that regulates the amount of glucose (sugar) in your blood. With diabetes, your body does not make enough insulin (type 1 diabetes), or it does not use it as it normally should. Common symptoms include being thirsty a lot, the need to frequently urinate, hunger, feeling very tired, and blurred vision. But there are also cases where, at least early in the disease, people do not have any symptoms at all. Some ethnic groups are at particular risk of getting type 2 diabetes. These include Native Americans, persons of Latin American backgrounds, Blacks, Native Hawaiians, Pacific Islanders, Arab Americans, and Asian Americans. At present, there's no known cure for type 2 diabetes. But the good news is that a large project called the Diabetes Prevention Program showed that people can avoid getting the disease if they include a healthy diet and physical activities into their lifestyle.

Vaccines are medications designed to stimulate the body's immune response against diseases. As such they are designed to prevent a disease from occurring (or becoming worse) rather than to treat an existing disease. As most recently demonstrated by the COVID-19 pandemic, some people are hesitant to use vaccines, believing them to be potentially harmful. Like almost any medical intervention, vaccines can have negative side effects. But the real issue is whether those side effects outweigh the potential harm (including death) a disease can cause.

REFERENCES

1. Abramitzky R. Boustan L. *Streets of Gold: America's Untold Story of Immigrant Success*. New York: Public Affairs.

2. Tayaben JL, Younas A. Call to action for advocacy of immigrant nurses during the COVID-19 pandemic. *Journal of Advanced Nursing*. 2020 Sep;76(9):2220-2221.

3. Shaffer FA, Bakhshi MA, Cook KN, Álvarez TD. The Contributions of Immigrant Nurses in the U.S. During the COVID-19 Pandemic: A CGFNS International Study. *Nurse Leadership*. 2021 Apr;19(2):198-203.

4. New American Economy Research Fund. *Building America: Immigrants in Construction and Infrastructure-Related Industries*. 09/03/2020. https://research.newamericaneconomy.org/report/covid19-immigrants-construction-infrastructure/

5. European Commission. *Immigrant Key Workers: Their Contribution to Europe's COVID-19 Response*. 04/24/2020. https://ec.europa.eu/migrant-integration/library-document/immigrant-key-workers-their-contribution-europes-covid-19-response_en

6. Littman RJ. Littman ML. Galen and the Antonine Plague. The *American Journal of Philology*. 1973, 94 (3):243–255.

7. Paul Rincon P. *Hun migrations linked to deadly Justinian Plague*. BBC News, 05/10/2018. https://www.bbc.com/news/science-environment-44046031

8. Thornton R, *American Indian Holocaust and Survival:* A Population History Since 1492. 1987 Norman: University of Oklahoma Press.

9. Barnett ED, Walker PF. Role of immigrants and migrants in emerging infectious diseases. *Medical Clinics of North America*. 2008 Nov;92(6):1447-58, xi-xii.

10. Soto SM. Human migration and infectious diseases. *Clinical Microbiology and Infection.* 2009 Jan;15 Suppl 1(Suppl 1):26-8.

11. Bhattacharya M, Dhama K, Chakraborty C. Recently spreading human monkeypox virus infection and its transmission during COVID-19 pandemic period: A travelers' prospective. *Travel Medicine and Infectious Disease.* 2022 Sep-Oct;49:102398

12. United States Drug Enforcement Agency. s. Rohypnol. https://www.dea.gov/factsheets/rohypnol

13. Centers for Disease Control and Prevention. *BCG-Vaccine Fact Sheet.* https://www.cdc.gov/tb/publications/factsheets/prevention/bcg.htm

14. National Institutes of Health. H-1B and O-1 Comparison Chart. 07/2020. https://ors.od.nih.gov/pes/dis/AdministrativeStaff/Documents/hocomparisonchart.pdf

15. Institute of Migration, World Migrant Report, 2022. https://worldmigrationreport.iom.int/world-migration-report-2022-selected-infographics

16. Batalova J. Top Statistics on Global Migration and Migrants. Migration Policy Institute. 07/21/2022. https://www.migrationpolicy.org/article/top-statistics-global-migration-migrants

17. Byju's the Learning App. Global Warming. https://byjus.com/biology/global-warming/

18. Rossati A. Global Warming and Its Health Impact. *International Journal of Occupational and Environmental Medicine.* 2017 Jan;8(1):7-20

19. McDonnell, T. *The Refugees the World Barely Pays Attention To.* National Public Radio. 06/20/2018.19. https://www.npr.org/sections/goatsandsoda/2018/06/20/621782275/the-refugees-that-the-world-barely-pays-attention-to

20. The Nansen Initiative. Disaster-Induced Cross-Border Displacement. 12/2015. https://disasterdisplacement.org/wp-content/uploads/2015/02/PROTECTION-AGENDA-VOLUME-1.pdf

21. World Health Organization, Nutrition, Stunting in a nutshell. 11/19/2015. https://www.who.int/news/item/19-11-2015-stunting-in-a-nutshell

22. United Nations Children's Fund (UNICEF): Malnutrition: Afghanistan's silent emergency. https://www.unicef.org/afghanistan/nutrition

23. Lyall, N & Shaar K. Three signs of impending famine in Syria absent immediate action. MEI@75 operations and Policy Center, 12/10/2021. https://www.mei.edu/publications/three-signs-impending-famine-syria-absent-immediate-action

24. The Food and Agriculture Organization of the United Nations, & The World Food Programme. (2021, July 30). *Hunger Hotspots: FAO-WFP early warnings on acute food insecurity* (August to November 2021 outlook).

25. Heller, S. Twelve Million Syrians Now in the Grip of Hunger, Worn Down by Conflict and Soaring Food Prices," World Food Programme (WFP), 17 February 2021. https://www.wfp.org/news/twelve-million-syrians-now-grip-hunger-worn-down-conflict-and-soaring-food-prices

26. Delgado, C, Smith, D, Stockholm International Peace Research Institute. 2021 Global Hunger Index: Hunger and Food Systems in Conflict Settings. https://www.globalhungerindex.org/pdf/en/2021.pdf

27. World Vision. *Forced to flee: Top countries refugees are coming from.* 06/18/2021. https://www.worldvision.org/refugees-news-stories/forced-to-flee-top-countries-refugees

28. Gavazzi G, Herrmann F, Krause KH. Aging and infectious diseases in the developing world. *Clinical Infectious Diseases.* 2004 Jul 1;39(1):83-91.

29. Worldometers. *Countries where COVID-19 has spread.* 01/05/2023. https://www.worldometers.info/coronavirus/countries-where-coronavirus-has-spread/

30. Cohn D'V, Horowitz JM, Minkin R, Fry R, Hurst K. *The demographics of multigenerational households.* Pew Research Center. 03/24/2022.

31. Generations United. *Multigenerational Households* https://www.gu.org/explore-our-topics/multigenerational-households/

32. Kolker, C. *The Immigrant Advantage: What we can learn from Newcomers to America about Health, Happiness, and Hope.* 2014, New York: Free Press

33. Lin JT, Mollan KR, Cerami C. The Consequences of Isolating at Home. *Clinical Infectious Diseases.* 2021 Nov 2;73(9):e2823.

34. Oum S, Kates J., Wexler A. Economic Impact of COVID-19 on PEPFAR Countries. KFF Global Health Policy. 02/07/2022 https://www.kff.org/global-health-policy/issue-brief/economic-impact-of-covid-19-on-pepfar-countries/

35. Migration Policy Institute. Fact Sheet. The Essential Role of Immigrants in the U.S. Food Supply Chain. 04/2020. https://migrationpolicy.org/content/essential-role-immigrants-us-food-supply-chain

36. World Health Organization. Tuberculosis Fact Sheet. 10/272022 https://www.who.int/news-room/fact-sheets/detail/tuberculosis

37. Cauthen GM, Pio HG, Ten Dam HG: *Annual risk of tuberculosis infection.* World Health Organization TB Publication 1988; 88:154

38. Bloom BR, Murray CJL: Tuberculosis: Commentary on a reemergent killer. *Science* 1992; 257:1055–1064

39. Menzies NA, Hill AN, Cohen T, Salomon JA. The impact of migration on tuberculosis in the United States. *International Journal of Tuberculosis and Lung Disease.* 2018. 01:22(12): 1392-1403

40. Oren E, Fiero MH, Barrett E, Anderson B, Nuñez M, Gonzalez-Salazar F. Detection of latent tuberculosis infection among migrant farmworkers along the US-Mexico border. *BMC Infectious Diseases.* 2016 Nov 3;16(1):630.

41. Boudville DA, Joshi R, Rijkers GT. Migration and tuberculosis in Europe. *Journal of Clinical Tuberculosis and Other Mycobacterial Diseases.* 2020 Jan 7;18:100143.

42. Phares CR, Liu Y, Wang Z, et al. Disease Surveillance Among U.S.-Bound Immigrants and Refugees — Electronic Disease Notification System, United States, 2014–2019. *Morbidity and Mortality Weekly Report*, Surveillance Summary 2022;71(No. SS-2):1–21.

43. US Centers for Disease Control and Prevention. *Title 42—The Public Health and Welfare.* https://www.govinfo.gov/content/pkg/USCODE-2011-title42/pdf/USCODE-2011-title42-chap6A-subchapII-partC-sec252.pdf

44. Duzkoylu Y, Basceken SI, Kesilmez EC. Physical Trauma among Refugees: Comparison between Refugees and Local Population Who Were Admitted to Emergency Department-Experience of a

State Hospital in Syrian Border District. *International Journal of Environmental Research and Public Health*. 2017;2017:8626275.

45. Al-Hajj S, Chahrour MA, Nasrallah AA, Hamed L, Pike I. Physical trauma and injury: A multi-center study comparing local residents and refugees in Lebanon. *Journal of Global Health*. 2021 Oct 9;11:17001.

46. Daily Beast. *Russians Accused of Raping and Killing a 1-Year-Old Child, Says Ukraine official.* https://www.thedailybeast.com/russians-accused-of-raping-and-killing-a-one-year-old-child-says-ukraine-official

47. Falk P. *UN told "credible" claims of sexual violence against children as Russia's war drives a third of Ukrainians from their homes.* CBS News. 5/13/2022

48. United Nations Security Council. *Sexual Violence 'Most Hidden Crime' Being Committed against Ukrainians, Civil Society Representative Tells Security Council.* 9056th Meeting. 06/06/2022. https://www.un.org/press/en/2022/sc14926.doc.htm

49. Al-Dayel N, Mumford A. ISIS and Their Use of Slavery. International Centre for Counter Terrorism. 27 Jan 2020 https://www.icct.nl/publication/isis-and-their-use-slavery

50. Sham M, Singh D, Wankhede U, Wadate A. Management of child victims of acute sexual assault: Surgical repair and beyond. *Journal of Indian Association of Pediatric Surgeons*. 2013 Jul;18(3):105-11.

51. Tahirbegolli B, Çavdar S, Çetinkaya Sümer E, Akdeniz SI, Vehid S. Outpatient admissions and hospital costs of Syrian refugees in a Turkish university hospital. *Saudi Medical Journal*. 2016; 37(7):809-12.

52. World Health Organization. *Ukraine's health system under severe pressure.* 06/03/2022. https://www.who.int/news/item/03-06-2022-one-hundred-days-of-war-has-put-ukraine-s-health-system-under-severe-pressure

53. The Soufan Center. *Syria: The Humanitarian-Security Nexus*, 2017, Author. https://thesoufancenter.org/research/syria-humanitarian-security-nexus-2/

54. Crespo E. The Importance of Oral Health in Immigrant and Refugee Children. *Children (Basel)*. 2019 Sep 9;6(9):102. https://www.mdpi.com/2227-9067/6/9/102

55. Salim NA, Tiwari T. Migrant and refugee Oral Health. *Community Dental Health.* 2021 Feb 25;38(1):3-4.

56. Ryan P, McMahon G. Severe dental infections in the emergency department. *European Journal of Emergency Medicine.* 2012 Aug;19(4):208-13.

57. World Health Organization Fact Sheet, Europe. *Migration and health: key issues.* January 20, 2021 https://www.who.int/europe/news-room/fact-sheets/item/migration-and-health-key-issues

58. The United Nations High Commissioner for Refugees. Data visualization on Mediterranean crossings charts rising death toll and tragedy at sea need UNHCR reference on deaths among migrants crossing the sea. 06/10/2022 https://www.unhcr.org/en-us/news/briefing/2022/6/62a2f90a1a/unhcr-data-visualization-mediterranean-crossings-charts-rising-death-toll.html

59. The United Nations High Commissioner for Refugees. Operational Data Portal. https://data.unhcr.org/en/situations/mediterranean

60. Bridges L. Central American Migrants Face Perils on Journey North. *North American Congress on Latin America (NACLA)* 05/24/2013. https://nacla.org/news/2013/5/24/central-american-migrants-face-perils-journey-north-0

61. Pardinas J (2008). Los retos de la migracion en Mexico: Un espejo de dos caras (PDF). *Serie Estudios y Perspectivas.* 99. Retrieved 3 June 2013.

62. Amnesty International Publications. *Invisible Victims: Migrants on the Move in Mexico.* 04/28/2010. https://www.amnesty.org/en/documents/amr41/014/2010/en/

63. NBC News. *Authorities ID 47 of the migrants found dead inside an abandoned truck in San Antonio.* 07/06/2022 https://www.nbcnews.com/news/latino/authorities-id-47-migrants-found-dead-abandoned-truck-san-antonio-rcna36931

64. Parker TJ, Moreno M. *5 people test positive for COVID after being found in suspected human smuggling operation in SW Houston, police say.* KTRK TV Houston. 04/30/2021. https://www.click2houston.com/news/local/2021/04/30/human-smuggling-happening-at-home-in-southwest-houston-kprc-2-sources-say/

65. Fox M. Migrants don't bring disease. In fact, they help fight it, report says. Migration also boosts economies, the new report notes. NBC News
https://www.nbcnews.com/storyline/immigration-border-crisis/
migrants-don-t-bring-disease-fact-they-help-fight-it-n944146

66. Becker J, Faller G. Arbeitsbelastung und Gesundheit von Erwerbstätigen mit Migrationshintergrund [Workload and health of workers with a migrant background]. *Bundesgesundheitsblatt Gesundheitsforschung Gesundheitsschutz.* 2019 Sep;62(9):1083-1091.

67. Moyce SC, Schenker M. Occupational Exposures and Health Outcomes Among Immigrants in the USA. *Current Environmental Health Reports.* 2017 Sep;4(3):349-354.

68. Yanar B, Kosny A, Smith PM. Occupational Health and Safety Vulnerability of Recent Immigrants and Refugees. *International Journal of Environmental Research and Public Health.* 2018 Sep 14;15(9):2004.

69. The Guardian: *Revealed: 6,500 migrant workers have died in Qatar since World Cup awarded.* 03/18/2021. https://
www.theguardian.com/global-development/2021/feb/23/
revealed-migrant-worker-deaths-qatar-fifa-world-cup-2022

70. Walter JD & Ford M. DW. Fact check: How many people died for the Qatar World Cup? *Deutsche Welle,* 11/16/2022
https://www.dw.com/en/fact-check-how-many-people-have-died-for-
the-qatar-world-cup/a-63763713

71. Jon Gambrell. Qatar Says Worker Deaths for World Cup 'Between 400 and 500' *Time Magazine* 11/29/2022.

72. Rai O A. A mysterious rash of kidney failures. *Nepail Times,* 04/2017. https://archive.nepalitimes.com/article/
Nepali-Times-Buzz/A-mysterious-rash-of-kidney-failures,3639

73. Zoni AC, Domínguez-Berjón MF, Esteban-Vasallo MD, Velázquez-Buendía LM, Blaya-Nováková V, Regidor E. Injuries Among Immigrants Treated in Primary Care in Madrid, Spain. *Journal of Immigrant and Minor Health.* 2018 Apr;20(2):456-464.

74. Dragioti E, Tsamakis K, Larsson B, Gerdle B. Predictive association between immigration status and chronic pain in the general population: results from the SwePain cohort. *BMC Public Health.* 2020 Sep 29;20(1):1462.

75. Centers for Disease Control and Prevention (CDC). *Diabetes risk factors.*
    https://www.cdc.gov/diabetes/basics/risk-factors.html

76. Joffe B, Zimmet P. The thrifty genotype in type 2 diabetes: an unfinished symphony moving to its finale? *Endocrine.* 1998 Oct;9(2):139-41.

77. Garduño-Espinosa J, Ávila-Montiel D, Quezada-García AG, Merelo-Arias CA, Torres-Rodríguez V, Muñoz-Hernández O. Obesity and thrifty genotype. Biological and social determinism versus free will. *Boletín Médico del Hospital Infantil de México.* 2019;76(3):106-112.

78. Diabetes Prevention Program (DPP) Research Group. The Diabetes Prevention Program (DPP): description of lifestyle intervention. *Diabetes Care.* 2002 Dec;25(12):2165-71.

79. World Health Organization, *Fact Sheet, Tobacco.* 05/24/2022.
    https://www.who.int/news-room/fact-sheets/detail/tobacco

80. Global Burden of Disease [database].Washington, DC: Institute of Health Metrics; 2019. IHME

81. Reimann JOF, Liles S, Hofstetter CR, Chu S, Angulo OY, Hovell, MF. *The popularity of cigars: continuing phenomenon or fading fad?* Poster Session B10, Annual Investigator's Meeting, Tobacco Related Disease Research Program. 1999
    http://trdrp.yes4yes.com/fundedresearch/grant_page.php?grant_id=380

82. Reimann JOF, Liles S, Rodríguez-Reimann, DI, Hovell, MF. *The new popularity of cigars: smokers descriptions.* Conference Paper, Annual Investigator's Meeting, Tobacco Related Disease Research Program. 1998

83. Truth Initiative, Fact Sheet, Cigars: Facts, stats and regulations. 06/30/2020.
    https://truthinitiative.org/research-resources/
    traditional-tobacco-products/cigars-facts-stats-and-regulations

84. Thirión-Romero I, Pérez-Padilla R, Zabert G, Barrientos-Gutiérrez I. Respiratory impact of electronic cigarettes and "low risk" tobacco. *Revista de Investigación Clínica.* 2019;71(1):17-27.

85. World Population Review. *Smoking Rates by Country 2022.*
    https://worldpopulationreview.com/country-rankings/
    smoking-rates-by-country

86. Statista. *Consumer Goods & FMCG›Tobacco. Share of individuals who currently smoke cigarettes, cigars, cigarillos or a pipe in selected European countries in 2020.*
https://www.statista.com/statistics/433390/
individuals-who-currently-smoke-cigarettes-in-european-countries/

87. CDC. Current Cigarette Smoking Among Adults in the United States. https://www.cdc.gov/tobacco/data_statistics/fact_sheets/adult_data/ cig_smoking/index.htm

88. El Hajj DG, Cook PF, Magilvy K, Galbraith ME, Gilbert L, Corwin M. Tobacco Use Among Arab Immigrants Living in Colorado: Prevalence and Cultural Predictors. *Journal of Transcultural Nursing.* 2017 Mar;28(2):179-186.

89. Joshi S, Jatrana S, Paradies Y. Tobacco smoking between immigrants and non-immigrants in Australia: A longitudinal investigation of the effect of nativity, duration of residence and age at arrival. *Health Promotion Journal of Australia.* 2018 Dec;29(3):282-292.

90. United States Public Health Service Office of the Surgeon General; National Center for Chronic Disease Prevention and Health Promotion (US) Office on Smoking and Health. *Smoking Cessation: A Report of the Surgeon General [Internet].* Washington (DC): US Department of Health and Human Services; 2020. Chapter 4, The Health Benefits of Smoking Cessation. https://www.ncbi.nlm.nih.gov/ books/NBK555590/

91. Crane T, Patterson S. *Introduction.* History of the Mind-Body Problem. 2001. pp. 1–2.

92. Catholic Answers. Dualism: Philosophical terms, employed in different meanings by different schools.
https://www.catholic.com/encyclopedia/dualism

93. Mehta N. Mind-body Dualism: A critique from a Health Perspective. *Mens Sana Monographs.* 2011 Jan;9(1):202-9.

94. Chan C, Ho PS, Chow E. A body-mind-spirit model in health: an Eastern approach. *Social Work in Healthcare.* 2001;34(3-4):261-82.

95. World Health Organization, WHO Director-General's opening remarks at the Mental Health at Work panel, World Economic Forum. 01/18/2023.
https://www.who.int/director-general/speeches/detail/

who-director-general-s-opening-remarks-at-the-mental-health-at-work-panel--world-economic-forum---18-january-2023

96. Rathod JM. Danger and Dignity: Immigrant Day Laborers and Occupational Risk. *Seton Hall Law Review*. 2016;46(3):813-82.

97. Arici C, Ronda-Pérez E, Tamhid T, Absekava K, Porru S. Occupational Health and Safety of Immigrant Workers in Italy and Spain: A Scoping Review. *International Journal of Environmental Research and Public Health*. 2019 Nov 11;16(22):4416.

98. Armstrong SA, Herr MJ. Physiology, Nociception. 2022 May 8. In: *StatPearls* [Internet]. Treasure Island (FL): StatPearls Publishing; 2022 Jan.

99. Colloca L, Ludman T, Bouhassira D, Baron R, Dickenson AH, Yarnitsky D, Freeman R, Truini A, Attal N, Finnerup NB, Eccleston C, Kalso E, Bennett DL, Dworkin RH, Raja SN. Neuropathic pain. *Nature Reviews Disease Primers*. 2017 Feb 16;3:17002.

100. Costigan M, Scholz J, Woolf CJ. Neuropathic pain: a maladaptive response of the nervous system to damage. *Annual Review of Neuroscience*. 2009. 32:1-32.

101. Lumley MA, Cohen JL, Borszcz GS, Cano A, Radcliffe AM, Porter LS, Schubiner H, Keefe FJ. Pain and Emotion: A Biopsychosocial Review of Recent Research. *Journal of Clinical Psychology*. 2011;67(9):942-968.

102. Institute of Medicine (US) Committee on Pain, Disability, and Chronic Illness Behavior; Osterweis M, Kleinman A, Mechanic D, editors. *Pain and Disability: Clinical, Behavioral, and Public Policy Perspectives*. Washington (DC): National Academies Press (US); 1987. 9, Psychiatric Aspects of Chronic Pain. Available from: https://www.ncbi.nlm.nih.gov/books/NBK219250/

103. Institute of Medicine (US) Committee on Advancing Pain Research, Care, and Education. *Relieving Pain in America: A Blueprint for Transforming Prevention, Care, Education, and Research*. Washington (DC): National Academies Press (US); 2011.

104. Chen Y, Mo F, Yi Q, Morrison H, Mao Y. Association between mental health and fall injury in Canadian immigrants and non-immigrants. *Accident Analysis & Prevention*. 2013 Oct;59:221-6.

105. Flores Morales J, Nkimbeng M. An Exploration of the Relationship Between Diabetes and Depression Among Immigrants in the

United States. *Journal of Immigrant and Minority Health.* 2021 Jun;23(3):444-451.

106. Black PH. The inflammatory response is an integral part of the stress response: Implications for atherosclerosis, insulin resistance, type II diabetes and metabolic syndrome X. *Brain, Behavior, and Immunity.* 2003;17;350-364.

107. Philis-Tsimikas A, Walker C, Rivard L, Talavera GA, Reimann JOF, Salmon M, Araujo R. Improvement in diabetes care of underinsured patients enrolled in Project Dulce: A community-based, culturally appropriate, nurse case management and peer education diabetes care model, *Diabetes Care,* 2004 27:110-115.

108. Concha JB, Kravitz HM, Chin MH, Kelley MA, Chavez N, Johnson TP. Review of type 2 diabetes management interventions for addressing emotional well-being in Latinos. *Diabetes Educator.* 2009 Nov-Dec;35(6):941-58.

109. Ilchmann-Diounou H, Menard S. Psychological Stress, Intestinal Barrier Dysfunctions, and Autoimmune Disorders: An Overview. *Frontiers in Immunology.* 2020 Aug 25;11:1823

110. Song H, Fang F, Tomasson G, Arnberg FK, Mataix-Cols D, Fernández de la Cruz L, Almqvist C, Fall K, Valdimarsdóttir UA. Association of Stress-Related Disorders With Subsequent Autoimmune Disease. *JAMA.* 2018 Jun 19;319(23):2388-2400.

111. Agrawal M, Shah S, Patel A, Pinotti R, Colombel JF, Burisch J. Changing epidemiology of immune-mediated inflammatory diseases in immigrants: A systematic review of population-based studies. *Journal of Autoimmunity.* 2019 Dec;105:102303.

112. Bookwalter DB, Roenfeldt KA, LeardMann CA, Kong SY, Riddle MS, Rull RP. Posttraumatic stress disorder and risk of selected autoimmune diseases among US military personnel. *BMC Psychiatry.* 2020 Jan 15;20(1):23.

113. Bustamante LHU, Cerqueira RO, Leclerc E, Brietzke E. Stress, trauma, and posttraumatic stress disorder in migrants: a comprehensive review. *Revista Brasileira de Psiquiatria.* 2017 Oct 19;40(2):220-225.

114. Schmeer KK, Tarrence J. Racial-ethnic Disparities in Inflammation: Evidence of Weathering in Childhood? *Journal of Health and Social Behavior.* 2018 Sep;59(3):411-428.

115. Joo JH, Platt R. The promise and challenges of integrating mental and physical health. International Review of Psychiatry. 2018 Dec;30(6):155-156.

116. Knowleswellness. *Banned Medicines in the United States.* 01/31/2022. https://www.knowleswellness.com/blog/ list-of-banned-medicines-in-the-united-states/

117. Kliegl, M. How to Transport Your Medicine to Europe, SAI. 01/06/2022 https://www.saiprograms.com/transport-medicine-europe/

118. Ramey JT, Bailen E, Lockey, RF. Rhinitis Medicamentosa. *Journal of Investigational Allergology and Clinical Immunology* 2006; Vol. 16(3): 148-155. https://www.jiaci.org/issues/vol16issue03/1.pdf

119. Hutchings MI, Truman AW, Wilkinson B. Antibiotics: past, present and future. *Current Opinion in Microbiology.* 2019 Oct;51:72-80.

120. Centers for Disease Control and Prevention. Antimicrobial Resistance. 12/17/2021. https://www.cdc.gov/drugresistance/index. html

121. World Health Organization. Wide differences in antibiotic use between countries. 11/12/2018. https://www.downtoearth.org.in/news/health/ wide-differences-in-antibiotic-use-between-countries-who-62096

122. University of Oxford, Medical Science Division. Global antibiotic consumption rates increased by 46 percent since 2000. 11/16/2021. https://www.medsci.ox.ac.uk/news/global-antibiotic-consumption-rates-increased-by-46-percent-since-2000

123. Mangione-Smith R, Elliott MN, Stivers T, McDonald L, Heritage J, McGlynn EA. Racial/ethnic variation in parent expectations for antibiotics: implications for public health campaigns. *Pediatrics.* 2004 May;113(5):e385-94. PMID: 15121979.

124. Mainous A.G., Cheng A.Y., Garr R.C., Tilley B.C., Everett C.J., McKee M.D. Nonprescribed antimicrobial drugs in Latino community, South Carolina. *Emerging Infectious Diseases.* 2005;11:883–888.

125. Céspedes A., Larson E. Knowledge, attitudes, and practices regarding antibiotic use among Latinos in the United States: Review and recommendations. *American Journal of Infection Control.* 2006;34:495–502.

126. FDA Authorizes Emergency Use of Novavax COVID-19 Vaccine, Adjuvanted. https://www.fda.gov/vaccines-blood-biologics/coronavirus-covid-19-cber-regulated-biologics/novavax-covid-19-vaccine-adjuvanted

127. U.S. Food & Drug Administration Coronavirus (COVID-19) *Update: FDA Limits Use of Janssen COVID-19 Vaccine to Certain Individuals.* 05/05/2022. https://www.fda.gov/vaccines-blood-biologics/coronavirus-covid-19-cber-regulated-biologics/janssen-covid-19-vaccine

128. CDC Fact Sheet, Tuberculosis https://www.cdc.gov/tb/publications/factsheets/general/tb.htm

129. Occupational Safety and Health Administration (OSHA). *The Bloodborne Pathogen Standard and the Enforcement Procedures for TB.* https://www.osha.gov/laws-regs/standardinterpretations/1997-09-23

130. Schwarcz J. Can Vaccines Make Our Body Magnetic? McGill Office for Science and Society. 06/11/2021. https://www.mcgill.ca/oss/article/covid-19/can-vaccines-make-our-body-magnetic

131. CDC. *Possible Side Effects After Getting a COVID-19 Vaccine.* 01/12/2022. https://www.cdc.gov/coronavirus/2019-ncov/vaccines/expect/after.html

132. Gamble VN. Under the shadow of Tuskegee: African Americans and health care. *American Journal of Public Health.* 1997 Nov;87(11):1773-8

133. Yasmin F, Najeeb H, Moeed A, Naeem U, Asghar MS, Chughtai NU, Yousaf Z, Seboka BT, Ullah I, Lin CY, Pakpour AH. COVID-19 Vaccine Hesitancy in the United States: A Systematic Review. *Frontiers in Public Health.* 2021 Nov 23;9:770985.

134. Gutiérrez Á, Young MT, Dueñas M, García A, Márquez G, Chávez ME, Ramírez S, Rico S, Bravo RL. Laboring With the Heart: Promotoras' Transformations, Professional Challenges, and Relationships With Communities. *Family & Community Health.* 2020; Dec 4.

135. Mendoza A. *Promotoras' playing role in vaccine outreach for Latino communities.* San Diego Union Tribune, 02/19/2021. https://www.sandiegouniontribune.com/news/health/story/2021-02-19/promotoras-play-important-role-in-vaccine-outreach-for-latino-communities

136. Afzal MM, Pariyo GW, Lassi ZS, Perry HB. Community health workers at the dawn of a new era: 2. Planning, coordination, and

partnerships. *Health Research Policy and Systems*. 2021 Oct 12;19(Suppl 3):103.

137. Department of Health Care Services (DHCS). Community Health Workers
https://www.dhcs.ca.gov/community-health-workers

138. Padilla R, Gomez V, Biggerstaff SL, Mehler PS. Use of curanderismo in a public health care system. *Archives of Internal Medicine*. 2001, 161(10):1336–1340.

139. Malruro, R. Curanderismo and Latino Views of Disease and Curing. *Western Journal of Medicine*. 1983 Dec; 139(6): 868–874.

140. National Center for Complementary and Integrative Health (NCCIH) *Ayurvedic Medicine: In Depth.*
https://www.nccih.nih.gov/health/ayurvedic-medicine-in-depth

141. AlRawi SN, Khidir A, Elnashar MS, Abdelrahim HA, Killawi AK, Hammoud MM, Fetters MD. Traditional Arabic & Islamic medicine: validation and empirical assessment of a conceptual model in Qatar. *BMC Complementary and Alternative Medicine*. 2017;17(1):157.

142. National Center for Complementary and Integrative Health (NCCIH) *Traditional Chinese Medicine: What You Need To Know*. 04/2019.
https://www.nccih.nih.gov/health/traditional-chinese-medicine-what-you-need-to-know

143. Bacardi-Gascon M, Dueñas-Mena D, Jimenez-Cruz A. Lowering effect on postprandial glycemic response of nopales added to Mexican breakfasts. *Diabetes Care*. 2007 May;30(5):1264-5.

144. Shapiro K, Gong WC. Natural products used for diabetes. *Journal of the American Pharmacists Association*. 2002; 42(2):217-226.

145. Chattopadhyay K, Wang H, Kaur J, Nalbant G, Almaqhawi A, Kundakci B, Panniyammakal J, Heinrich M, Lewis SA, Greenfield SM, Tandon N, Biswas TK, Kinra S, Leonardi-Bee J. Effectiveness and Safety of Ayurvedic Medicines in Type 2 Diabetes Mellitus Management: A Systematic Review and Meta-Analysis. *Frontiers in Pharmacology*. 2022 Jun 8;13:821810.

146. Vickers AJ, Vertosick EA, Lewith G, MacPherson H, Foster NE, Sherman KJ, Irnich D, Witt CM, Linde K; Acupuncture Trialists' Collaboration. Acupuncture for Chronic Pain: Update of an Individual Patient Data Meta-Analysis. *The Journal of Pain*. 2018; 19(5):455-474.

147. Zhang Q. Traditional and Complementary Medicine in Primary Health Care. In: Medcalf A, Bhattacharya S, Momen H, et al., editors. *Health For All: The Journey of Universal Health Coverage.* Hyderabad (IN): Orient Blackswan; 2015. Chapter 12. https://www.ncbi.nlm.nih.gov/books/NBK316267/

148. California Board of Psychology Laws and Regulations. https://www.psychology.ca.gov/laws_regs/2019lawsregs.pdf

149. World Health Organization. Global Standards for Quality Health-Care Services for Adolescents. https://apps.who.int/iris/bitstream/handle/10665/183935/9789241549332_vol1_eng.pdf

150. Sekhar MS, Vyas N. Defensive medicine: a bane to healthcare. *Annals of Medical and Health Sciences Research.* 2013;3(2):295-296. United States Drug Enforcement Agency. *Fact Sheets. Rohypnol* https://www.dea.gov/sites/default/files/2020-06/Rohypnol-2020_0.pdf

151. Jakulin, A. *Why are we such a litigious society? Statistical Modeling, Causal Inference, and Social Science*, Columbia University. https://statmodeling.stat.columbia.edu/2015/12/03/why-us-litigious/

152. Justpoint. US Medical Malpractice Case Statistics. 2017-2021 https://justpoint.com/knowledge-base/us-medical-malpractice-case-statistics

153. Almeida LM, Caldas J, Ayres-de-Campos D, Salcedo-Barrientos D, Dias S. Maternal healthcare in migrants: a systematic review. *Maternal and Child Health Journal.* 2013 Oct;17(8):1346-54.

154. Missing Migrants Project. https://missingmigrants.iom.int/

155. Woman, unborn child die after migrants abandoned in truck near U.S.-Mexico border. Border Report. 03/07/2022. https://www.borderreport.com/news/health/woman-unborn-child-die-after-migrants-abandoned-in-truck-near-u-s-mexico-border/

156. Maru S, Glenn L, Belfon K, Birnie L, Brahmbhatt D, Hadler M, Janevic T, Reynolds S. Utilization of Maternal Health Care Among Immigrant Mothers in New York City, 2016-2018. *Journal of Urban Health.* 2021 Dec;98(6):711-726.

157. Kentoffio K, Berkowitz SA, Atlas SJ, Oo SA, Percac-Lima S. Use of maternal health services: comparing refugee, immigrant and US-born populations. *Maternal and Child Health Journal.* 2016;20(12):2494–2501.

158. Gissler M, Alexander S, MacFarlane A, Small R, Stray-Pedersen B, Zeitlin J, Zimbeck M, Gagnon A. Stillbirths and infant deaths among migrants in industrialized countries. *Acta Obstetricia et Gynecologica Scandinavica.* 2009;88(2):134-48.

159. Fair F, Raben L, Watson H, Vivilaki V, van den Muijsenbergh M, Soltani H; ORAMMA team. Migrant women's experiences of pregnancy, childbirth and maternity care in European countries: A systematic review. *PLOS One.* 2020 Feb 11;15(2):e0228378.

160. Van Norman GA. Drugs and Devices: Comparison of European and U.S. Approval Processes. *JACC: Basic to Translational Science.* 2016 Aug 29;1(5):399-412.

161. Last Christmas, Universal Pictures. 2019. https://www.universalpictures.com/movies/last-christmas

162. Patricia Frye Walker PF & Barnett ED. *Immigrant Medicine.* 2007 Amsterdam, Netherlands: Elsevier Inc.

163. Berry JW. Acculturation. In the *Encyclopedia of Applied Psychology,* 2004; 27-34. Academic Press, Elsevier: Amsterdam.

164. Reimann JOF, Rodríguez-Reimann DI. *Immigrant Concepts: Life Paths to Integration.* 2021, Chula Vista CA. Romo Books.

165. Berry, JW. Theories and models of acculturation. In S. J. Schwartz & J. B. Unger (Eds.), *Oxford library of psychology. The Oxford handbook of acculturation and health, 2017;* (p. 15–28). Oxford University Press.

166. Voelker, R. Born in the USA: Infant Health Paradox. *JAMA: The Journal of the American Medical Association.* 1994 272 (23): 1803–1804.

167. Speciale AM, Regidor E. Understanding the Universality of the Immigrant Health Paradox: The Spanish Perspective. *Journal of Immigrant and Minority Health.* 2011, 13 (3): 518–525

168. Guendelman, S; Abrams, B. Dietary intake among Mexican-American women: generational differences and a comparison with white non-Hispanic women. *American Journal of Public Health.* 1995 85 (1): 20–25

169. Antecol, H, Bedard, K. Unhealthy Assimilation: Why Do Immigrants Converge to American Health Status Levels? *Demography.* 2006 43 (2): 337–360.

170. Rodríguez-Reimann DI, Nicassio P, Reimann JOF, Gallegos PI, Olmedo EL. Acculturation and health beliefs of Mexican Americans regarding tuberculosis prevention. *Journal of Immigrant Health,* 2004: 6:51-62.

171. Becker MH, Maiman LA. Sociobehavioral determinants of compliance with health and medical care recommendations. *Medical Care* 1975; 13:10–24.

172. Reimann JOF, Ghulam M, Rodríguez-Reimann DI, Beylouni MF. Project Salaam: Assessing mental health needs among San Diego's greater Middle Eastern and East African communities. *Ethnicity & Disease*, 2007, 17, Supp. 3, S3-39-S3-41. PMID: 17985449

173. Gonzalez-Guarda RM, Stafford AM, Nagy GA, Befus DR, Conklin JL. A Systematic Review of Physical Health Consequences and Acculturation Stress Among Latinx Individuals in the United States. *Biological Research for Nursing*. 2021 Jul;23(3):362-374.

174. Andrasfay T, Goldman N. Reductions in 2020 US life expectancy due to COVID-19 and the disproportionate impact on the Black and Latino populations. *Proceedings of the National Academy of Sciences USA*. 2021 Feb 2;118(5):e2014746118.

175. U.S. Health & Human Services, Office of Minority Health. *The National CLAS Standards*. https://minorityhealth.hhs.gov/omh/browse. aspx?lvl=2&lvlid=53

176. National Association of Social Workers, *Standards and Indicators for Cultural Competence in Social Work Practice*. https://www.socialworkers.org/LinkClick. aspx?fileticket=PonPTDEBrn4%3D

177. American Hospital Association. *Becoming a Culturally Competent Health Care Organization*. https://www.aha.org/system/files/hpoe/Reports-HPOE/becoming-culturally-competent-health-care-organization.PDF

178. Barbara McAneny BL, How I incorporated cultural competency in my practice. *American Medical Association*. 03/22/2015 https://www.ama-assn.org/about/leadership/ how-i-incorporated-cultural-competency-my-practice

179. Centers for Disease Control and Prevention. *Cultural Competence In Health And Human Services*. https://npin.cdc.gov/pages/ cultural-competence

180. Purnell, L. The Purnell Model for Cultural Competence. *The Journal of Multicultural Nursing & Health*, Summer 2005, 7-15

181. Albougami AS, Pounds KG Alotaibi JS. Comparison of Four Cultural Competence Models in Transcultural Nursing: A Discussion Paper. *International Archives of Nursing and Health Care*; 2016, Volume (2)4

https://clinmedjournals.org/articles/ianhc/international-archives-of-nursing-and-health-care-ianhc-2-053.pdf

182. Reimann JOF, Talavera GA, Salmon M, Nuñez J, Velasquez RJ. Cultural competence among physicians treating Mexican Americans who have diabetes: A structural model. *Social Science & Medicine*. 2004; 59:2195-2205.

183. Yepes-Rios M, Reimann, JOF, Talavera AC, Ruiz de Esparza A, Talavera GA. (2006) Colorectal cancer screening among Mexican Americans at a community clinic. *American Journal of Preventive Medicine*, 30, 204-210.

184. Shiu-Thornton S, Balabis J, Senturia K, Tamayo A, Oberle M. Disaster preparedness for limited English proficient communities: medical interpreters as cultural brokers and gatekeepers. *Public Health Reports*. 2007 Jul-Aug;122(4):466-71.

185. Office of the Surgeon General (US); Center for Mental Health Services (US); National Institute of Mental Health (US). Mental Health: Culture, Race, and Ethnicity: A Supplement to Mental Health: A Report of the Surgeon General. Rockville (MD): Substance Abuse and Mental Health Services Administration (US); 2001 Aug. Chapter 2 Culture Counts: *The Influence of Culture and Society on Mental Health*. Available from: https://www.ncbi.nlm.nih.gov/books/NBK44249/

186. Hampton NZ, Sharp SE. Shame-focused attitudes toward mental health problems. *Rehabilitation Counseling Bulletin*. 2013; 57:170–81.

187. Haque A. Mental health concepts in Southeast Asia: diagnostic considerations and treatment implications. *Psychology, Health & Medicine*. 2010 Mar;15(2):127-34.

188. Mascayano F, Tapia T, Schilling S, Alvarado R, Tapia E, Lips W, Yang LH. Stigma toward mental illness in Latin America and the Caribbean: a systematic review. *Brazilian Journal of Psychiatry*. 2016 Mar;38(1):73-85.

189. Amuyunzu-Nyamongo M. *The social and cultural aspects of mental health in African societies* Commonwealth Health Partnerships 2013 5 https://www.commonwealthhealth.org/wp-content/uploads/2013/07/The-social-and-cultural-aspects-of-mental-health-in-African-societies_CHP13.pdf

190. Uono S, Hietanen JK. Eye contact perception in the West and East: a cross-cultural study. *PLOS One*. 2015 Feb 25;10(2):e0118094.

191. Reimann JOF, Ghulam M, Rodríguez-Reimann DI, Beylouni MF. *Bringing communities together for wellness: An assessment of emotional health needs among San Diego's Middle Eastern, North African, and East African groups*. 2005, San Diego: ICSD.
192. Brach C., & Fraser, I. Can cultural competency reduce racial and ethnic health disparities? A review and conceptual model. *Medical Care Research Review*, 2000, 57,(Supp. 1), 181-217.
193. Weiler D, Crist JD, Diabetes Self-Management in the Migrant Latino Population. *Hispanic Health Care International*, 2007 5(1), 27-33.
194. National Educational Association. Policy Brief. Global Competence Is a 21st Century Imperative. https://www.girlbossmath.com/uploads/1/1/7/5/117585876/nea_global_imperative.pdf
195. World Savvy. What is Global Competence? https://worldsavvy.org/static/e77c2d687176df004f1bbde66f1e8a76/Global-Competence-Matrix-2023.pdf
196. Dyches C, Haynes-Ferere A, Haynes T. Fostering Cultural Competence in Nursing Students Through International Service Immersion Experiences. *Journal of Christian Nursing*. 2019 Apr/Jun;36(2):E29-E35.
197. Larson KL, Ott M, Miles JM. International cultural immersion: en vivo reflections in cultural competence. *Journal of Cultural Diversity*. 2010 Summer;17(2):44-50.
198. Mews C, Schuster S, Vajda C, Lindtner-Rudolph H, Schmidt LE, Bösner S, Güzelsoy L, Kressing F, Hallal H, Peters T, Gestmann M, Hempel L, Grützmann T, Sievers E, Knipper M. Cultural Competence and Global Health: Perspectives for Medical Education - Position paper of the GMA Committee on Cultural Competence and Global Health. *GMS Journal for Medical Education*. 2018 35(3):1-17.
199. Reimann, JOF, Rodríguez-Reimann, DI. *Community based health needs assessments with culturally distinct populations*. In A. Pelham & E. Sills (Eds.) Promoting Health & Wellness in Underserved Communities: Multidisciplinary Perspectives through Service-Learning Series (pp.82-100), 2010, Sterling, VA: Stylus Publishing.
200. Giddings LS & Grant BM. Mixed methods research for the novice researcher. *Contemporary Nurse*, 2006 23:3-11.
201. Access Community Health & Research Center https://www.accesscommunity.org/health-wellness/medical

202. World Health Organization. Monkeypox outbreak, 2022
https://www.who.int/emergencies/situations/
monkeypox-oubreak-2022

203. US Department of State, Exchange Visitor Program
https://j1visa.state.gov/

204. Martin N. Germany looks abroad for nurses, caregivers. *Deutsche Welle (DW)* 08/14/2020.
https://www.dw.com/en/
germany-looks-abroad-for-nurses-caregivers/a-54576126

205. Maaroufi M. Precarious Integration: Labour Market Policies for Refugees or Refugee Policies for the German Labour Market? *Refugee Review* Fall 2017 3:15-33.

206. Ziegler J. *US-educated doctors are sued for malpractice twice as frequently.* United Press International, 03/11/1986.

207. Global Skills Partnership. Center for Global Development.
https://www.cgdev.org/page/global-skill-partnerships

208. Khan Y, O'Sullivan T, Brown A, Tracey S, Gibson J, Genereux M, et al. Public health emergency preparedness: a framework to promote resilience. *BMC Public Health.* 2018, 18:1344.

209. Sushil M, Sharma K, Yogesh D, Gupta K, Kumar Y. Mass media for health education: a study in the State of Rajasthan. *Multidisciplinary International Journal.* 2017. 1:26–39.

210. Erlandson RA. Role of Electron Microscopy in Modern Diagnostic Surgical Pathology. *Modern Surgical Pathology.* 2009:71–84.

211. Hall N, Schmitz HP, Dedmon JM. Transnational Advocacy and NGOs in the Digital Era: New Forms of Networked Power, *International Studies Quarterly.* 2020 64(1):159–167.

212. Lurie SG. Global Health Equity and Advocacy: The roles of international Non-Governmental Organizations. *Health, Culture, and Society.* 2012, 2(1):104-114.

213. Gundersen C, & Ziliak, JP. Food Insecurity and Health Outcomes. *Health Affairs*, 2015, 34(11): 1807.

INDEX

"f" after a page number indicates a figure

THE *IMMIGRANT STRIDES TOWARD PROSPERITY* SERIES

BOOK 1

"The authors' practical advice, combined with their academic backgrounds and humanitarian empathy, makes for a definitive work on immigration that convincingly counters the simplistic "zero-sum game" analysis that too often surrounds debates on the issue."

— Kirkus Reviews

BOOK 2

"This book stands as an urgent intervention, illuminating crucial distinctions, laying out new approaches, and encouraging greater understanding. A valuable resource offering psychological context for those who work with immigrant populations."

— BookLife, *Publishers Weekly*

BELOW ARE EXCERPTS FROM OUR FIRST AND SECOND BOOKS IN THE SERIES.

References and endnotes have been removed from this text for clarity, but can be found in the original books.

FROM *IMMIGRANT CONCEPTS: LIFE PATHS TO INTEGRATION*

THE GROUP FOR IMMIGRANT RESETTLEMENT & ASSESSMENT (GIRA)

...our work as psychologists often entails forensic evaluations for immigration cases (e.g., extreme hardship cases; asylum applications; spousal abuse cases, etc.). In a different but related field, we have conducted university-based public health and psychological research. Both research and clinical services have largely focused on culturally and linguistically distinct populations (particularly Latino, East African, and Middle Eastern immigrants and refugees). This work is ongoing. Such efforts are rewarding in that they can positively impact a variety of people.

In short, we are always ready for a new project. Each is an adventure. For us, the present questions are: How do we use our experience in some additional constructive way? Can we help create systematic approaches that aid immigrants in their efforts to acclimate to a new country? If so, how do we do that? Is there a methodical approach that people who work with immigrants will find useful?

These questions prompted us to form the Group for Immigrant Resettlement & Assessment (GIRA) several years ago. GIRA is a multidisciplinary entity made up of clinical and social psychologists, researchers, career development specialists, leaders of community-based organizations, and others who have relevant expertise. Our group's mission is to create, and then use, psychometric measures that add relevant information to immigration processes that allow for informed choices when helping immigrants. In this context, our interest is in professional, nuanced, and non-political approaches that contribute to solutions in these types of circumstances.

As clinicians or social service providers, we generally listen to our clients' needs and circumstances to come up with an individualized assistance (or treatment) plan. GIRA's effort is essentially the same. It includes development of an instrument, the Successful Immigrant Resettlement Inventory (SIRI), which assesses primary dimensions discussed in this book and uses that information to identify an individual's unique needs and circumstances.

Specifically, SIRI includes basic demographic information and then addresses acculturative/psychosocial stressors, openness to acculturative and adaptive processes, psychological and behavioral tendencies (including personality traits and resilience), physical health status, and employment/career orientations. Both immigrants and people who help them can then use this information to develop a comprehensive and personalized roadway to success.

We further believe that this type of measurement can have uses that assist legal procedures used in immigration cases. For example, asylum seekers often lack documents that "prove" their difficult history. Verifying psychological symptoms that are consistent with trauma-related disturbances can add credibility to legitimate asylum seekers.

In short, SIRI can act as an assessment and service planning tool used by a non-governmental organization (NGOs) community-based organizations (CBOs), government entities, educational systems, and others. With results in hand, people who work on the front lines can help immigrants by identifying and using the right services. This approach can enhance and enable a smoother acculturative process by assisting people to overcome acculturative and resettlement barriers. For example, a SIRI report has the potential to enhance the quality of life and positive social contributions by developing effective employability/educational plans for immigrants who need this type of help.

On a broader level, information from SIRI can inform policy. It can pinpoint what types of services are most needed in specific areas and for specific people. That can then help us put money and other resources where they will do the most good.

At the same time, assessing immigrants in multiple ways can also raise difficult questions. What if there are people with criminal and even terrorist risk factors in the group? SIRI is not a measure that can spot a terrorist in a crowd. But, if applied properly, it may point to ways in which radicalization risks, particularly among people who feel they have no future, can be lowered.

Many people, especially from Middle Eastern, North African, and other predominantly Muslim countries hesitate to talk about radicalization, and for good reasons. They are worried about being stereotyped because that has happened to them. Many have been victims of terrorists themselves. So they know the dangers involved firsthand. Yet, in their adopted country they are often grouped in with the very people they have fled from. That has to be perplexing at best. Similarly, there are far too many public comments about people from Mexico and Central America that label the actual victims of criminals as "the" criminals.

Never-the-less, there can also be some real concerns. While a very small number of immigrants are criminals and/or terrorists, we only need to consider the history of attacks in the US, the UK, Spain, France, Austria, and many other countries to know that a few radicals can cause a lot of death and destruction. Given this reality, we need to better understand what the facts around radicalization are. Is there a substantial relationship between criminal acts and immigration? Who is most tempted to join criminal/terrorist groups? Are there things we can do to divert people from such decisions?

Criminal Activity Among Immigrants

Arguably, the amount of criminal activity among foreign-born persons is less than that among the native-born population in several countries. Information from the US Bureau of Justice Statistics shows that non-citizen inmates in state and federal prisons comprise less than 6% of the total prison population. Alex Nowrasteh, director of immigration studies at the Cato Institute has concluded that "the criminal conviction and arrest rates for immigrants (even in case of the undocumented) were well below those of native-born Americans." An overall analysis of 51 US studies published on the subject from 1994–2014 found that, if anything, immigration tends to be associated with reduced rather than increased crime rates. The reasons for this trend remain poorly understood. But there is substantial evidence that it has been consistently true in recent history.

Research on this topic in other countries across the world has shown mixed results. No relationship between immigration status and crime has, for example, been found in Australia. In Italy, studies found that foreign-born persons tended to commit slightly more robberies from 1990–2003. But the overall crime rate among non-native residents then dropped by 65% between 2007 and 2016. Similarly in the UK, one study noted that the local prison population was not increasing substantially due to any incidents of a serious crime committed by foreign persons.

On the other hand, research in Germany, Norway, Spain, and a few other countries have reported higher crime rates attributed to immigrants, though in some instances these increases were relatively small.

Is there a way to fix things if crime rates are a problem? Some studies in the EU have found that granting legal status to undocumented persons can reduce crime. This may happen because legal status opens up more economic opportunities and generally reduces fears and frustrations for people.

Crimes Against Immigrants

On the other side of this picture is the concern that immigrants are too often the victims rather than the perpetrators of crime. People fleeing from war and persecution can be quite vulnerable to abuse and exploitation. For example 75% or more Syrian refugees are at-risk women and children. Even if they make it to refugee camps, many fear they will be abused by staff and others there. Some female refugees end up being sexually exploited under the premise that this is the only way they can survive financially.

Closely related to this situation is sex trafficking. The American Civil Liberties Union (ACLU) reports that in the US, almost all victims of sex trafficking are immigrant women with an average age of 20 years. Women with less education, limited English speaking ability, and no knowledge of US legal employment protections are particularly at risk.

Other parts of the world also report the victimization of immigrants. One study in South Africa, for example, found that 85% of the foreign-born people they assessed had been victims of crimes. The most common crimes were break-ins of homes and lootings of immigrant businesses.

Additional types of criminal activity encountered by immigrants include being robbed while migrating and experiencing hate crimes. Yet our research as well as other studies shows that victims rarely report such incidents to authorities for fear of drawing attention to themselves and being victimized even more.

Radicalization and Terrorism

Terrorism is constantly in the news. While the number of people involved is relatively small, we all know that one person who commits a violent act can create havoc for many others. Yet, as previously noted, is also true that based on their religion and dress, some immigrant groups are too often stereotyped across the board as "terrorists."

The actual relationship between immigration and terrorism has not been sufficiently researched. A 2016 study did find that higher levels of migration were associated with a lower level of terrorism in the host country. At the same time, migrants who are specifically from terror-prone states do increase the risk of terrorism in the host country. Some of these latter findings may not even involve foreign-born persons. When we were at a 2019 conference in London we, for example, heard anecdotal concerns that ISIS fighters, who had been driven from their territory in Syria, were coming to the UK. But these were not necessarily "foreigners." Some were UK passport holders who were returning "home."

The topic of radicalization is highly complex. First, it is important to note that the expression of "radical" or "extremist" beliefs does not automatically mean the person or persons involved are going to commit violence. In fact, among some nations including the US, the expression of radical ideas, without the threat of or advocacy for violence, is protected in the Constitution. Secondly, violent terrorist acts have been committed in the name of multiple causes. These include homegrown as well as international roots. The August 3, 2019, mass shooting in our old hometown of El Paso, Texas was not perpetrated by immigrants but was prompted by anti-Mexican hate. In addition, the US Federal Bureau of Investigation (FBI) called growing domestic violent extremism the number one terrorist threat in 2021.

To counter violent radicalism, we need to understand terrorists' motivations, attitudes, world views, and thought processes. "Understanding" doesn't excuse or find rationales for their behaviors. Rather, the well-worn Sun Tzu quote: (paraphrasing) "know yourself, know your enemy, and you shall win a hundred battles" without loss points to the wisdom of identifying what we are facing to find effective counters. Behavioral scientists (e.g., psychologists) have much to contribute but have been underutilized in this effort.

What are some basics in understanding radicalization? First, it is important to know that radical extremists do not all fit one profile. Those in recruitment and leadership positions are, for example, unlikely to go on suicide missions themselves though they try to attract others who are willing to do so. Secondly, terrorism is not necessarily connected with mental disorders though that tends to be a common presumption.

But there are some known risk factors. Those who are susceptible to recruitment by terrorist groups often lack self-confidence and feel themselves to be rejected by greater society. They believe that they have no path to a good future. Then along comes a recruiter who promises them belonging, a type of family and brotherhood, and a central role in the creation of a great and just new world. Even if they die they are promised 1) rewards in the afterlife and 2) that they will be remembered as a martyr. Finally, some radical groups promise to take care of the family members after a "martyr's" death. This "sales pitch" can be profoundly attractive to someone who feels he or she belongs nowhere and has no future.

What can be done to counter this kind of radicalization risk? One of the most interesting views we have heard is from the Soufan Center. Rather than a social service organization, this group is largely made up of law enforcement and intelligence professionals who have worked in national and international agencies.

The Soufan Center's 2017 publication "Syria; The Humanitarian Security Nexus" argues that, for refugees, humanitarian and security concerns cannot be addressed separately. Rather, they are two faces of the same coin. People who have hope for acceptance, opportunities, and a positive future are much more able to resist the false promises made by radical groups. This can not only help immigrants themselves but can have positive ripple effects for their children and children's children. Social and behavioral scientists have echoed similar themes by emphasizing that positive social and community connections, support, and cooperation can help thwart violent extremism.

Providing multi-faceted, organized, integrated, and coordinated avenues for immigrants can offer them a ladder to earned success. Support and guidance is a constructive rather than punitive action. But it requires that we have a good up-front assessment of peoples' needs and circumstances. GIRA seeks to foster such an assessment.

Questions to Consider

- If you were the victim of a crime would you feel comfortable notifying the police or other authorities? If not, what law enforcement actions would give you more confidence that reporting a crime would have a good outcome for you?
- Do you feel that you have been subjected to prejudice and hate?
- What allows you to persevere, even if you have had negative experiences?

Resources

Many organizations help members of radical groups that have become disillusioned and want to leave that life. These organizations treat both international terrorists and local right-wing hate groups.

To find out more about countering violent extremism, please see a review of the topic at: https://www.mei.edu/publications/deradicalization-programs-and-counterterrorism-perspective-challenges-and-benefits.

FROM *IMMIGRANT PSYCHOLOGY: HEART, MIND, AND SOUL*

ENVIRONMENTAL STRESSORS AND PSYCHOLOGICAL CONSEQUENCES

Acculturative Stress

People migrate for many reasons; some for professional advancement in highly specialized occupations. Others do so to escape poverty and secure a better future for their children. Some migrate to escape war, persecution, climate change, and violence.

Despite the varied motives, migrants share one thing in common: Moving to a new home tends to cause stress. Even under the best of circumstances, learning new customs and a new language is challenging for most. At minimum personal routines, sleep cycles, and established habits are disrupted.

Especially among people fleeing war and persecution, there can be several stressors. These fall into three general categories. First, people may have undergone traumatic events such as war, torture, assault including rape, and the loss of loved ones in their country of origin.

Secondly, there is the stress of the journey itself. For refugees and others fleeing poverty, migrating often means traveling through several countries and sometimes languishing in refugee camps for months or even years. The journey may lead them through places where they are not welcome and are abused. Common abuses include forced labor, sexual exploitation, extortion, and robbery. The following three examples illustrate such journeys.

Regular paths among Middle Eastern refugees have led them from Syria to Libya, and then on to Europe. East African refugees from Somalia often escape to Kenya or Ethiopia before reaching their final destinations. Many people from Central America go through Mexico to reach the US. In such travels, the exploitation of children, including unaccompanied minors, is of particular concern since they are a highly vulnerable population.

Secondly, even under positive circumstances, trips can involve several stops, each of which requires some adaptation to new circumstances. But, as recently demonstrated along the US-Mexico border, acceptance into the country of final destination is far from guaranteed.

Third is the need to adapt to the new country's particular milieu. This can require people to learn routine skills such as understanding new road signs and driving on a different side of the street. But more complex challenges such as learning a new language and adapting to different educational systems, job requirements, laws, and customs are common.

Given these conditions, it is not surprising that the scientific and clinical literature acknowledges acculturative stress (also sometimes called immigration stress and relocation stress syndrome) as needing serious attention and solutions.

These types of difficulties have consequently been listed in formal diagnostic books that identify psychological problems. Both the American Psychiatric Association's Diagnostics and Statistical Manual of Mental Disorders, Fifth Edition (DSM-5) and the International Classification of Diseases, Tenth Edition (ICD-10) listed "acculturation difficulty" in its terms. The ICD-10 described such difficulty as being a "problem with migration" and a "problem with social transplantation."

What mental health challenges can be part of acculturation stress? Anxiety, worry, depression, loneliness, and in some severe cases, substance abuse are all taxing mental health symptoms associated with the process of adapting to an unfamiliar country. All these stressors interfere with a person's ability to connect with others, making the situation even worse. It is, however, worth mentioning that not all cases are severe. Some people may only experience mild tensions which improve over time.

Acculturation stress can also show itself through physical symptoms. In part, this is because anxiety is often connected with physiological responses such as shortness of breath and chest pains. (Later in this book we discuss the physical symptoms of anxiety in detail.) Both anxiety and depression can also cause unhealthy increased or decreased activity in the heart and blood vessels. Changes in appetite and the use of prescribed (as well as other) drugs can also cause physical difficulties.

In addition, emotional symptoms, combined with physical reactions, can leave people more susceptible to other diseases because of decreased immunity. Problems can become increasingly worse because people in distress may not take care of themselves. The process causes a cycle in which physical and emotional problems interact, magnify each other, and make both worse. In short, acculturation stress impacts a complex set of physical and mental conditions.

A lack of access to healthcare services also exacerbates mental and physical health issues. Even moving to a new state or city in the same country can mean changes in healthcare providers and sometimes insurance coverage. So moving to a new country may add language barriers and unfamiliarity with healthcare policies and systems, further complicating acculturative stress.

How common is acculturation stress? It varies greatly across different populations and circumstances. The exact statistic is not well known. But it is notable that, as per one estimate, the prevalence of more severe posttraumatic stress disorder (PTSD) among migrants is very high (47%). This is particularly true for refugees. PTSD is mentioned here because, while it is not automatically the same as acculturative stress, there is frequent overlap between the two.

Who is most at risk? Perhaps it comes as no surprise that acculturation stress levels are connected with the degree to which a new country is similar to, or different from, an immigrant's country of origin. This includes the new culture's political system and social attitudes. In short, when a new culture is quite different from a newcomer's native culture, greater acculturative stress is likely to be experienced.

Immigrants who are highly sought after due to professional expertise and/or whose physical features, language, traditions, and religions are similar to the local majority population will probably have an easier time acculturating. On the other hand, immigrants who look "different" and/or who face lower economic circumstances tend to have greater adaptive difficulties. They are more likely to face negative stereotypes and attitudes from natives of the country toward the newcomers.

Some immigrants also have professional knowledge and expertise that is not accepted in their new country (e.g., foreign-trained attorneys and healthcare providers) and thus have educational and professional obstacles to overcome. This includes becoming familiar with local rules and practices. In some cases, it also means getting licenses to practice in a new county. Depending on where someone migrates from, the acceptance of a foreign professional education in a new country (and then gaining licensure in that country) can be quite difficult.

Another factor contributing to acculturative stress is whether a person's migration was voluntary or not. According to one source, involuntary migrants experience about 50% more acculturative stress than those who left their country of origin under more positive circumstances.

Undocumented immigrants also tend to experience substantial acculturative stress. A lack of legal papers restricts their ability to work, makes them more vulnerable to exploitation (such as working in hazardous conditions for low wages or becoming a victim of sex trafficking), and often leaves them fearful of immigration raids. The outcome of such raids can separate families. Some members are deported, and others are not. This can be quite common. United States data from 2017, for example, estimated that there were 16.7 million families that included both documented and undocumented relatives living in the same household. Almost six million were US-born children. In addition, 4.4 million children under age 18 live with at least one undocumented parent. An estimated half-million children who are US citizens experienced the deportation of at least one parent between 2011 and 2013.

Not surprisingly, separations due to deportation are painful and difficult for those being deported and often distressing for the family members left behind. This can be particularly severe in the case of children. An Immigration Council report cites links between parental deportation and emotional disturbances. This included stress that can impair brain development, create poorer educational outcomes, and generate involvement with child welfare systems among minors.

> **Case Example from Joachim Reimann:**
> While it did not involve children, one example illustrating problems generated by deportation from our clinical practice is as follows: A US-born husband had

to move to Tijuana, Mexico, and traveled over the border each day to be with his undocumented wife—even though he was an active-duty member of the US Armed Forces. The husband had a particular concern for the safety of both him and his family. There had been multiple kidnappings for ransom in Tijuana, and he believed that his military status made him a "high-value target" for such crime.

Later in this book, we will cover how documentation of psychological issues can be helpful in the legal process. But for now, it is sufficient to say that the procedures involved are long, convoluted, and difficult making them quite stressful.

As noted above, children and adolescents are not immune from acculturative stress. It can be generated by a host of reasons including the family's legal status, and whether the migration was forced by war or criminal threats because such occurrences are often connected with lower economic security.

But there is also good news. For years, especially since 1986, researchers have noted that some immigrant populations actually have *better* physical and mental health than the broader population in which they live. Asian, Latino, and Caribbean immigrants, for example, experience lower rates of mental illness than their non-immigrant counterparts. Given the economic and other stressors many immigrants face, this fact may seem counterintuitive. As such it has been labeled the "epidemiological paradox," "Hispanic paradox" or "immigrant paradox."

What accounts for these unexpected trends? One element may be that many people who migrate (regardless of the specific reason) tend to be hearty. They are willing to give up the old and familiar for the new and largely unknown. In addition, you have to be pretty healthy to undergo (and survive) long, complex, and potentially dangerous journeys. Immigrants also bring healthy parts of their culture with them. This includes their traditional diets that exclude unhealthy fast foods, the amount of physical activity they engage in, and close, supportive family networks.

Multiple generations living in one household can also be helpful. While a more crowded home can be a source of COVID-19 spread during that pandemic, studies have found that, among West Indian and Latin American immigrant groups, multi-generation households help increase homeownership, emotional support among family members, and practical benefits such as more readily available childcare.

In addition, religion can have a positive impact. One study of women from Latin American countries reported that acculturative stress was less when they had greater religious faith. While not a complete solution, prayer, and other faith-based meditation, regardless of specific beliefs, can decrease stress.

Other studies have found that a desire to acculturate is helpful. This can be caused by an understanding that a return to a migrant's country of origin is not desired or viable.

Children and adolescents have both advantages and disadvantages. They tend to learn languages faster than their adult counterparts and adapt more readily to new environments than adults. This can have both positive and negative outcomes. Negatives include the potential to upset traditional roles around power and authority in the family. Children and adolescents may end up with more responsibilities in negotiating the new country. By necessity, they often find themselves in the role of guides and interpreters for their parents. While practically useful, such roles can clash with traditional norms, cause resentment among family members, and impose responsibilities that children are not developmentally ready for.

But over the long run, quicker acculturation is likely to be helpful for these children as they mature. For example, in a study that looked at Latino/a adolescents' language acquisition and success in broader society, those who had learned more English had more positive experiences across many aspects of their new home. Yet, as previously mentioned, quicker acculturation can also impose family conflicts and unhealthy types of dependence.

To summarize, factors that can cause immigrants to be more vulnerable to acculturative stress are:

1. Experiences of trauma in their country of origin and/or during their travels to a new country;
2. Experiences of discrimination and non-acceptance in the new country;
3. Negative changes in socioeconomic status and/or ongoing poverty;
4. Older immigrants who have more difficulties learning new customs and a new language;

Factors that can protect against acculturative stress include:

1. Similarities between the country of origin and new country cultures;
2. If the same language is common in the country of origin and the new country;
3. The immigrant has skills and expertise that are highly valued in the new country;
4. The immigrant is physically similar (in terms of racial and ethnic features) to the majority population in the new country and thus tends to "blend in;"

5. Immigrants have strong social and family support systems.

Trauma: Rape, Torture, and Other Injury

As previously noted, a history of traumatic experiences is, unfortunately, all too common among migrants who are forced to flee their native country and who have few economic means. This section explores the subject of trauma among immigrants in greater detail.

The exact number of immigrants who experience trauma in 1) their country of origin, 2) during the migration journey, 3) in their adopted country, or 4) in some combination of these settings is not well known. Records from governments and other organizations are often sparse or non-existent. Immigrants can also be hesitant to report traumatic incidents, fearing that doing so will bring them unwanted attention. But there is some information we do have.

For example, immigrants undergoing forced migration and those without legal status are at particular risk for trauma. A 2018 Washington Examiner report noted 2,200 deaths, 180,000 rapes, and coerced sex, 81,000 cases of being forced to smuggle drugs, and 27,000 cases of human smuggling during a single year.

Some statistics from specific locations are as follows: Migration to the US. from Mexico and Central America has been substantial for many years. A report by the Center for Immigration Studies states that among the migrants from Central America's Northern Triangle (Honduras, Guatemala, El Salvador) 68.3% reported being victims of violence. In addition, 38.7% said that they underwent two such incidents and 11.3% cited three incidents. Violent encounters can occur in both a migrant's country of origin and on the journeys to their destinations.

Specific violent episodes included various types of physical assaults and sexual abuse. Seven percent (7%) of these migrants reported that they had been shot. Perpetrators of violence during migrants' journeys included criminal gangs and members of local security forces.

In addition, many incidents of exploitation were reported. This included extorting monetary bribes as well as demanding sex as payment for travel, protection, and shelter. In our clinical practice, we have heard of girls as young as 13 years old who were sexually exploited, some of whom were impregnated.

Notably, people crossing the US–Mexico border are not only from Latin American countries. Some originated in the Middle East and other locations. Anecdotally we have heard that a well-traveled route starts with a trip to a European country. For migrants with economic means, this is followed by a flight to Mexico City or another major city in Mexico, presumably because entrance requirements there are more relaxed. People then take a local flight to a US-Mexico border city like Ciudad Juarez or Tijuana, Mexico. Finally, they present themselves as asylum seekers to US border authorities or simply try to cross on their own. The number of people who've traveled such routes and experienced traumatic events is unknown. But given that they have fled their homes, most likely because they were under some form of threat there, it is presumed to involve substantial numbers.

A few statistics from Europe are available. The European Union Agency for Fundamental Rights (FRA) acknowledges that most EU government agencies do not collect information around traumatic experiences. But among its member states Greece's Asylum Services reported that, in 2016, 577 of its applicants were registered as having survived torture, rape, or other sexual violence. Most of these were from Syria, Iraq, and Afghanistan.

While clear statistics are again sparse, the FRA has also reported that police and other officials have employed excessive-use-of force and related abuses against immigrants arriving in Europe. Specific incidents include using unleashed dogs, pepper spray, beatings, verbal intimidation, and taking away warm clothing. Countries involved as perpetrators have included Hungary, Bulgaria, and Greece.

In our research among San Diego's Middle Eastern and East African populations, we found that a majority of immigrants (56%) reported that they had undergone some form of persecution in their countries of origin. Of these 17% had been tortured, most commonly because of their religious beliefs and/or cultural and tribal origins. Another 37% acknowledged having encountered some form of harassment in the US. This included hate crimes. Our clinical experiences show that the circumstances we found have not abated to any major degree over time.

Our clinical work has also included services with people who reported experiencing torture. Some incidents were perpetrated by individuals and brutal criminal groups. Others involved organized state-sponsored torture that followed a systematic protocol and had a political motivation.

One typical example from a Middle Eastern country is as follows: Individuals were picked up by local authorities and accused of sedition against the government. They were most often from minority religious and/or ethnic groups and may have refused to join the governing political party. Most often they were not part of an organized resistance group, possibly because such organizations have better means to protect their members.

The individuals were incarcerated and put in a dark cell where they were isolated but could hear screams of other inmates who were presumably being tortured. They were largely denied food and toilet facilities. They were then repeatedly interrogated and beaten. In one case we are aware of, the male inmate's mother was detained, stripped naked, and beaten in front of him. Individuals were also taken out to a courtyard and told they would be killed there. After repeated beatings, intimidation, isolation, and threats of death, people were given a way out of the prison. Specifically, they were told that they needed to make a written confession of their (often non-existent) crimes against the government and agree to spy on their family members, friends, and neighbors if they wanted to be released. They then had to report any presumably suspicious activities to the government. Not surprisingly, individuals often agreed to these terms so they could leave the prison.

Some who have undergone this torture then flee the country. This process is also fraught with political dangers. Some are caught without documentation in another country and sent back home. There they are seen as having violated their "agreement" and as having fled, both circumstances that can lead to even harsher punishment including death. In addition, some people may have cooperated with their captors before fleeing abroad. They may then be identified as perpetrators of violence and viewed as one of the "bad guys" by their fellow migrants.

Unresolved Grief

Not surprisingly, incidents and circumstances like the ones described above often lead to profound grief and loss. This is our next topic.

Migrant Deaths: One source of psychological distress for some immigrants and their families is the experience of grief. Many have lost loved ones to war, persecution, gang violence, and other incidents. Others may not know if lost or kidnapped family members are still alive. Such events can happen, both in an immigrant's country of origin and on the journey to a new location. If these circumstances are not resolved, a severe problem clinically known as "complicated grief" can develop.

The chances of death among people traveling to a new country can be substantial. There is no way to be certain about the exact number of people who have lost their lives during the immigration process. Many of these incidents are not recorded. But several international organizations and local initiatives have tried to document them. Here are some estimates.

On a global level, more than 75,000 migrant deaths have been recorded since 1996. Such statistics not only highlight the issue of migrant fatalities but can also shed light on the potential impact these incidents may have on family members who are left behind.

The International Organization of Migration (IOM) Missing Migrants Project is one effort to track migrant statistics. The IOM combines data from many different sources and uses that to record the deaths of people during the international migration process. It also includes migrants who have gone missing while traveling over bodies of water (mostly in boats) on their journey. From a practical and policy view, this can help identify deaths occurring at various borders, pinpointing especially dangerous routes. The numbers do not, however, typically include deaths that occur in refugee camps, detention facilities, during deportation, or when migrants were forced to return to their place of origin.

Recent trends from the IOM's data show the worldwide deaths or disappearances of more than 33,400 women, men, and children since the organization began to collect such information in 2014. The majority of these deaths (18,500) have been in the Mediterranean Sea. The central Mediterranean route from North Africa to Italy accounts for the highest number of these deaths and disappearances, claiming 15,500 lives between January 2014 and October 2019.

More than 7,400 deaths have also been recorded across the African continent. Many of these occurred when people attempted to cross the Sahara Desert. In addition, more than 3,000 deaths have been attributed to migrations in Asia, most recently linked to migrations from Myanmar by the Rohingya people (an ethnic group in the region).

In Central America, more than 3,600 people have been reported missing during a migration since 2014. Roughly 60% of these numbers were documented on the US-Mexico Border.

Migrant deaths can become particularly "real" and shocking when they happen close to home, even when they don't involve people one knows. On the morning of May 2, 2021, as we were writing this book in San Diego County, a 40-foot cabin cruiser with an estimated 30 undocumented migrants on board, hit a reef in rough waters and broke apart at one of our local beaches. Despite intense rescue efforts, at least four people died and many more were hospitalized. The boat was reportedly unsafe— the primary goal for smugglers is profit, not human life. What happens to the people is largely irrelevant to them if they've made their profits.

Such incidents are hardly uncommon. In November of 2021, twenty-seven migrants drowned while trying to cross the English Channel from France to the UK. Their overloaded inflatable boat capsized. The dead reportedly included five women and a little girl. People from Africa and Middle Eastern countries evidently see the UK as the best destination for them because English is spoken there, some already have relatives in the UK, and it is easier for them to get jobs due to a more relaxed approach to employment and immigration laws.

The IOM's Missing Migrants Project is important for several reasons. Statistics it generates can be used by governments to assess the risks of common migration routes and then design policies and programs to make the process safer. The project also supports persons who are searching for lost loved ones by making referrals to the Restoring Family Links Network operated by the Red Cross and Red Crescent.

It probably comes as no surprise that the circumstances described above can lead to emotional distress among immigrants. The next section addresses the forms such distress can take.

Complicated Grief: When considering the numbers cited above, it is easy to see that grief, bereavement, and in its more severe form, complicated grief, are common problems among immigrants. As such they are often treated by psychologists, psychiatrists, and other mental health professionals who work with these populations.

Most people experience the distress of losing a loved one at some point in their lives. For the vast majority of us normal grief and bereavement involves a period of sorrow, sadness, detachment, and even guilt and anger over the loss. People will likely continue to miss and remember their loved ones. But, in time, the emotional intensity connected with the loss will become less. This is a natural healing process.

When people work through bereavement, they usually experience different stages of the grieving process. The exact order and duration of each phase varies from person to person.

As per Kübler-Ross, grieving typically begins with denial that the loss is real. This is often followed by anger at the unfairness of the loss. This anger can be aimed at people who are seen as having caused the loss or as self-blame. Some also become very depressed, feeling that hope for a better life is gone. Many people ultimately come to accept a loved one's death. They experience the reality of the loss. But they also adjust to their new lives, plans, and dreams for the future. Finally, people can be hopeful and gain new healthy relationships.

In cases where a death is caused by violence or criminal acts, people can also find solace if they believe that the perpetrator has been brought to justice. Some may ultimately find it in themselves to forgive the offender.·

But for others, a loss is so devastating that their emotional distress does not end or even decrease over time. Clinically we understand this experience as "complicated grief" or "persistent complex bereavement disorder." In such cases, painful emotions and loss remain so severe and long-lasting that it is exceedingly difficult for the person to recover and go back to a "normal life."

Let us consider the similarities and differences between common grief and more complicated grief: As previously noted, ordinary experiences among grieving people include sorrow and sadness over the loss of your loved one(s). This state becomes worse when the bereaved encounters places, people, and situations that remind them of the person(s) they lost.

At first, the difference between common bereavement and complicated grief is hard to confirm. During the first few months after a loss, many symptoms connected with normal grief and complicated grief are the same. But, while normal grief symptoms gradually start to fade over time, those of complicated grief remain or get worse.

Some indicators of complicated grief are as follows: People continue to experience intense sorrow, pain, and worry over the loss of their loved one. They also continue to feel an intense longing for the deceased loved one. There is little focus on anything else but the loved one's death. There is a strong reaction to places, individuals, and circumstances that are reminders of the loved one and are avoided because of the intense grief they stir.

People with complicated grief can also experience feelings of detachment and emotional numbness. They begin to have a sense of bitterness about their loss, believing that their life no longer holds meaning or purpose. They appear unable to enjoy anything or think back on positive memories they shared with their lost loved one. Often, they begin to distrust others who, in their opinion, "cannot possibly understand" the experience as the mourner does.

The problems that arise from complicated grief can be severe and long-lasting. People in this category have a reduced ability to think of anything but their grief, and experience difficulties accepting a loved one's death. Anger and bitterness about the death may cause them to lose hope in life. Engaging in activities that were routine before the loss grows increasingly difficult and people with complicated grief. They withdraw from other people, feel guilty for not having been able to prevent a loved one's death, and concluded that life is not worth living anymore. They often wish that they had died with their loved one. Some may even consider suicide. In addition, people may experience physical symptoms associated with anxiety. These can include shortness of breath and chest or other body pains.

Stress can also weaken the immune system, increasing the risk for physical illness (for example, heart disease, cancer, or high blood pressure). There can be substantial overlap between grief and posttraumatic stress disorder (PTSD). We discuss PTSD in detail below.

Mental health experts do not fully understand why some people who have been exposed to similar circumstances develop complicated grief while others do not, but several factors may be involved. These include a genetic predisposition, the acquired methods for coping with the world, and type of personality.

Older people and women appear to be more vulnerable and at risk of developing complicated grief. Other circumstances that increase people's chances of developing such grief include an unexpected or particularly violent death (for example a car accident, murder, war, or suicide), the death of a child, having been very dependent on the deceased person, a loss of friendships (for example when others blame the grieving person for the death), a history of other trauma and/or emotional disorders, and additional stress in life.

Researchers do not have much information about the prevalence of complicated grief among specific national groups. However, one study reported that, while it depends on the country where people are from, the most common estimate is that 32% of immigrants experience such grief. Immigrants' grief can be increased when important family members are not present to help and the life in a new country limits the degree to which traditional burial practices can be followed.

One key to diagnosing and treating grief and complicated grief is to recognize the cultural and religious contexts that frame an individual's experience. But even when someone encounters similarities across a person's cultural and religious background, there are always individual differences that need to be considered and respected.

In summary, complicated grief can have a physical, mental, and social impact on immigrants. Those who have had to flee their homes due to war, poverty, and criminal violence are at particular risk. They often undertake long and dangerous journeys. Some basic considerations in dealing with grief are described below. This is followed by a discussion about resilience against complicated grief.

When to Ask for Professional Help: Some people may be reluctant to seek professional services because they fear that they will be judged and ridiculed. This can be due to friends and family members who have critiqued the grief behaviors ("It has been a while; you should be finished with it by now"). But mental health professionals are more aware that each person needs to grieve at their own pace and in their own time.

Nevertheless, it is a good idea to contact your doctor or a mental health professional if you have intense grief and problems functioning. The time people take to grieve varies greatly. People should not be afraid to seek help. Certainly, if emotional distress does not improve within one year, seeking professional treatment is advisable.

How to prevent complicated grief is not entirely clear. Seeking counseling soon after a loss may help, especially for people at increased risk of developing complicated grief. We address various formal treatments later in this book. But here are some initial thoughts on ways that may make grief more manageable.

- **Talking:** When people can talk about their grief and allow themselves to show their emotions (such as crying). This can reduce the chance of being overwhelmed by their sadness. Crying is one way our bodies handle and discharge stress.

- **Support:** In ideal circumstances, family members, friends, social support networks, and faith communities can all help people work through their grief. Some support groups focus on a particular type of loss, such as the death of a spouse or a child during war. Experiencing people in similar circumstances who have progressed in the grieving process can demonstrate that getting better is possible.

- **Culture-based coping:** While death is universal, various cultures have found different ways to deal with loss and grief. For example, the Day of the Dead (November 1 & 2) (*Día de Los Muertos*) is a Mexican holiday which has overlap with the Catholic celebrations of All Saints' Day and All Souls' Day as observed in many countries. This holiday allows family and friends to remember and honor their deceased by celebrating their lives. People build home altars, make offerings, and visit graves with gifts. This practice is not the same as but has some overlap with ancestor veneration as practiced in the Chinese Taoist tradition. It is based on the belief that deceased family members continue to exist; their spirits look after the family and influence the fortune of the living. It is up to the living family members to keep the ancestors happy in the spiritual world. Both of these examples are rituals and beliefs that honor and remember the deceased with joy rather than focusing on the loss of their death. In part, that serves to reinforce the continuity of the family line.

Clients sometimes teach us quite a bit about coping and resilience when we are conducting therapy. Here is one such example from our practice.

Case Example from Joachim Reimann:

A patient came to our office in emotional distress. She had escaped political persecution in an Eastern European country and had been successful in establishing a new life in the US. She had, for example, married and planned to have children. But then her new husband died in an accident.

This young woman described herself as having had the ability to control her emotions under usual circumstances. But she had lost that power when her husband died. Poignantly, she recounted an incident during which a co-worker had told her that it was "amazing you survived." Without thinking, she replied: "I didn't." She had not been in the accident herself. So she had no physical injury. The woman's response was about her psychological functioning.

Ultimately the young woman turned out to be both right and wrong in her response. She did not remain exactly as she had been before her husband's accident. It changed her. Therefore, her former self did not in fact, survive. But in time she was able to honor her husband's memory by living the life she knew he would want her to have. By her description, he clearly loved her and wanted the best for her. So, she set out to make that happen.

Posttraumatic Stress Disorder

Most psychologists, psychiatrists, and other mental health service providers use standard diagnoses found in the latest International Classification of Diseases or, in the US, the

Diagnostic Statistical Manual to figure out what their patients might be suffering from. This helps us to decide how to best treat them.

Posttraumatic stress disorder (PTSD) is one such diagnosis. It is generally defined as a mental condition that can occur if a person directly experienced or personally witnessed one or more traumatic event(s) or learned that such event(s) happened to a loved one or experienced repeated or extreme exposure to adverse details of one or more such events.

PTSD includes symptoms such as intrusive thoughts about the trauma, "flashbacks," problems sleeping, nightmares, significant anxiety, feelings of unreality or detachment from others, agitation/irritability, startle responses, depression, problems concentrating, and physical reactions to situations that remind people of trauma they have experienced. Later in this section, we go into greater detail about the various experiences people with PTSD tend to have.

We suspect it comes as no surprise that PTSD can be a problem for immigrants who have experienced very grievous events such as war, persecution, criminal threats, extortion, sexual assault, physical injuries, and other ordeals. Specific estimates have varied from roughly 30% among Syrian adults to a high of 76% among Syrian children. One study found that 9% of Latin American immigrant adolescents and 21% of their caregivers were at risk for PTSD. This compares to between 1% and 6% who have PTSD in the general adult population across the world.

US military forces withdrew from Afghanistan while we were writing this book. The exact psychological impact of this event on the Afghan population is still unknown. But news reports constantly showed crowds of desperate people at the Kabul airport trying to leave the country between August 14 and 31, 2021. Overall, combined efforts by the US and its allies evacuated more than 114,000 people to various nations after the Taliban takeover. All indications are that people will continue to flee the new regime. Thus, it is highly probable that host countries taking in Afghan refugees will see a high number of immigrants with PTSD in this population.

The personal stories of Afghan refugees are often both frustrating and inspiring. A May 13, 2022, article in *The Week*, for example, describes members of the Female Tactical Platoon, an elite Afghan military unit that supported US Special Forces in tracking down Taliban fighters. As women, they could gather intelligence from other women more easily. By all accounts, the women were very successful in their missions. But with the US withdrawal, they had to flee their homes. As per the article, at least one was then working at a fast-food place in the US. Given their proven skill, determination, courage, and support of US objectives, it appears likely that the Female Tactical Platoon veterans will more than succeed in their new lives. But it also behooves their new country to recognize proven talent and help further these women's success.

As previously mentioned, Russia's invasion of Ukraine has created another situation in which many fled and continue to flee their home. As we write this book the ultimate outcome of the war remains unknown. But it illustrates that a refugee crisis can impact people from all socioeconomic backgrounds. It is further notable that, depending on the conflict's resolution, many Ukrainians may also wish to return home and rebuild their country rather than becoming permanent immigrants in other nations. Whether the flight from Ukraine is temporary or will cause a permanent shift in host-country populations thus remains an open question. But it seems likely that many Ukrainian refugees will suffer from PTSD.

History and Cultural Contexts: Relationships between traumatic events and subsequent "nervous" or psychological symptoms have been noticed throughout human history. These relationships have had labels such as *sustos*, (soul loss or soul fright) in Latin American cultures, and *khyâl* (wind) attacks in Cambodian traditions.

In Western societies what is now called PTSD has had multiple prior labels. In the 19th Century, they included "nervous shock." In the military realm of the era, early 1870s US Civil War records also describe a condition called "soldier's heart" or "irritable heart" connected to combat stress. Then in World War I, a condition called "shell shock" was described. During the Second World War, the term "shell shock" was gradually replaced by "combat neurosis." Other labels at various times have been "terror neurosis" (*schreckneurose*), "acute neurotic reaction," "triggered neurosis," "post-accident anxiety syndrome," and "posttraumatic hysteria." During the US-Vietnam conflict "battle fatigue" was frequently discussed. Finally, in 1980 "posttraumatic stress disorder" became the official term for this problem.

Why do some people develop psychological difficulties from trauma and others do not? Genetic, physical, and social factors make some people more susceptible to developing PTSD after a traumatic experience. The combination of past trauma and ongoing long-term stressors can worsen symptoms and may be particularly common among people who have undergone hazardous forced migrations. This is referred to as complex PTSD in the scientific literature. In one of our studies, we for example found that immigrants from the Middle East and East Africa who had experienced multiple traumas in their lives had more severe symptoms than those who did not have such experiences. Given this type of evidence, complex PTSD will probably be considered for inclusion in future editions of the International Classification of Diseases.

In summary, the criteria, paraphrased from the DSM-5 used to diagnose PTSD and supplemented with some immigrant-specific examples are:

A. The person has experienced an event that threatened his or someone else's death, serious injury, or sexual violence in one (or more) of the following ways:

1. The person has directly experienced a traumatic event or events. Among people who have had to flee their country of origin (and/or are en route to a new country), this can include being injured, raped, tortured, robbed, or harmed in some other way.

2. The individual has personally witnessed the event(s) as it happened to others such as friends or family members. This, again, is a common experience among people who have undergone forced migrations.

3. The person has learned that one or more traumatic events happened to a close family member or close friend. Such event or events must have been physically or psychologically violent. Some people, for example, learn that loved ones have been killed, kidnapped, or lost so their status and whereabouts are unknown. At times people will never learn what happened to their loved ones.

4. The person repeatedly hears about or sees details involved in the traumatic event or events. For example, people may see the remains of a loved one even if they did not see the death itself, or repeatedly hear the details of a loved one's

death or severe injury from others. Media coverage of the Ukraine war which shows murdered civilians lying in the street is one sad example.

B. One (or more) of the following symptoms associated with the traumatic event or events are experienced:

1. Repeated, unwanted, and distressing memories of the traumatic event or events. People try to avoid these memories but often can't do so.

2. Repeated distressing dreams which are related to the traumatic event or events.

3. Experiences in which a person feels or acts as if the traumatic event was occurring again. In extreme cases, people may become so overwhelmed by such experiences that they are not aware of their actual surroundings at the time.

4. Intense or long psychological distress when experiencing sensations, seeing places or hearing things that remind people of their traumatic experience(s). This can, for example, include loud noises that sound like explosions felt during war, and news reports of accidents or disasters.

5. Notable physical reactions to circumstances that symbolize or resemble an aspect of the traumatic event(s) a person has experienced. This can include increased heart rate, sweating, nausea, and other physical symptoms.

C. A constant tendency to avoid various reminders connected with the traumatic event or events. This can be one or both of the following:

1. People with PTSD tend to make (often unsuccessful) efforts to avoid distressing memories, thoughts, or

feelings that are in some way connected with the traumatic event(s).

2. People with PTSD tend to make efforts to avoid reminders such as persons, places, situations, and other circumstances that produce distressing memories of the trauma they have experienced.

D. Negative changes in thoughts and mood connected with the traumatic event(s). These begin or worsen after the traumatic event(s) have happened, and include two more of the following challenges:

1. Difficulties remembering some details of the traumatic event(s) (although other details can be quite vivid.) In this case, it is presumed that problems thinking and remembering are not caused by head injury, alcohol or drugs, or other psychological issues.

2. Constant and exaggerated beliefs and expectations (for example that "I'm a bad person," "The bad things that happened were my fault," "People in the world cannot be trusted," "The world is completely unsafe")

3. Constant, inaccurate thoughts about the cause and/or results of the traumatic event or events that lead people to blame themselves or others.

4. Persistent fear, horror, anger, guilt, or shame.

5. A lack of desire to participate in activities that were previously enjoyable. Sometimes that can involve almost complete withdrawal from others.

6. Feeling disconnected from other people including friends and relatives.

7. A constant inability to feel positive emotions such as satisfaction or love.

E. Increased and large negative reactions that start or worsen after experiencing one or more traumatic events. This usually involves two or more of the following:

1. Ill-tempered behavior or angry outbursts (for little or no reason) are typically expressed as verbal or physical attacks toward people or objects.

2. Reckless or self-destructive behavior. (This is particularly true for children who have PTSD.)

3. Hypervigilance. (This is a state of increased alertness. People experiencing PTSD are extremely alert to hidden dangers even though there may be no real threats.)

4. Amplified startle responses. People with a trauma history tend to get easily surprised and frightened by unexpected noises or movements.

5. Problems concentrating. (Many people with severe PTSD are so focused on their disturbing thoughts about past trauma they have trouble paying attention to their current surroundings. They may express this condition as "memory problems." But the truth is, a person can't remember what they couldn't concentrate on to begin with.)

F. Substantial problems sleeping, including nightmares, caused by difficult and unwanted thoughts about trauma.

G. The duration of the problems listed above is more than 1 month. If it is less than one month a different diagnosis called "acute stress disorder" applies.

H. The disturbance causes substantial distress and/or problems for people in social situations on the job, or in other activities of daily life. Some people, for example, become so withdrawn and disoriented that they cannot go shopping, get lost when they go out of their home, and need others to help them with most routine activities.

I. The previously described symptoms were not caused by a substance (for example: medications, alcohol, recreational drugs) or other medical conditions. Some people use drugs in an effort to cope with problems. Certainly, self-medicating with drugs or alcohol can create its own problems (like paranoia). Research has shown that the combination of PTSD and substance abuse is common in immigrant populations. But to diagnose PTSD, substance abuse (or a substantial increase in such abuse) should be in response to a traumatic experience.

It is important to note that some people acting in some form of self-defense, may have committed violence. In this case, they can suffer from consequent psychological trauma. For example, children who are forced to be soldiers may have felt they had no choice in the matter. Even adults in civilian life may have experienced situations in which they committed violence under threat to keep themselves from being attacked. In short, trauma experiences do not always entail a clear distinction between "victims" and "perpetrators." These two categories can overlap. As previously noted, people who were forced to fight others or be killed themselves may flee the situation and then be identified as enemies by their fellow immigrants. This makes for complex legal and moral issues.

While PTSD is caused by environmental experiences, it can produce physical changes in the brain. How the trauma-exposed brain then automatically reacts when it perceives danger tends to change. For example, researchers have looked at the way our brains recognize threats. In people who have experienced trauma, the primitive part of the brain sees dangers everywhere which can cause dramatic reactivity. In contrast, people without a substantial trauma history tend to interpret things as more manageable. Overall, traumatic experiences tend to change how we perceive dangers, how we decide what is unsafe enough to warrant a strong response, and how we respond (both in terms of our actions and physical sensations) to perceive threats.

As a result, people with PTSD have trouble filtering out situations that, in practical reality are not very threatening. The habit of automatically being distressed by unexpected events is formed. Having experienced dangerous and unpredictable circumstances, people become easily startled (by, for example, someone walking up behind them). As mentioned in the previously discussed diagnostic criteria for PTSD they are often particularly "triggered" by reminders of past trauma. This is not necessarily a voluntary thought-out reaction but involves automatic "fight or flight" responses in more basic parts of the brain (e.g., the amygdala) In short, the brain bypasses rational analysis and goes directly from relative calm to an extreme fear that may not be commensurate with the level of real danger. People with such experiences are usually overly vigilant as they anticipate and create ways to prevent the next catastrophe.

Another common reaction to trauma is anger. The US National Center for PTSD described it as a "*core piece of the survival response in human beings.*" In dangerous situations, it can give us the energy necessary to stay alive. But if angry responses become a habit, they cause obvious problems in our lives.

There are clues when people are reacting to something in their past that they have not come to terms with. They often talk in absolutes—commonly using the words "*never*" and "*always.*" Minor difficulties are perceived as extreme. They tend to see themselves as victims rather than survivors. Anxiety is regularly met with anger and rage. The good news is that research suggests positive thoughts can also result in better physical brain functioning. In other words, there is hope that we can overcome problems, even in our physical brain.

This book would be incomplete without mentioning vicarious trauma. Such trauma refers to emotional reactions by healthcare providers, social service workers, border security personnel, immigration specialists (e.g., attorneys, interpreters), and others who hear about the difficult events people they come in contact with have undergone. Certainly many healthcare providers, especially in hospital settings, have felt such trauma during the COVID-19 pandemic as they treat an overwhelming number of sick and dying patients day after day. Similarly, people who work with refugees can feel such trauma as they hear about and see the consequences of war, torture, and other horrific experiences.

A somewhat related concept is intergenerational trauma. This entails trauma reactions that are passed down from those who directly experience the original events to following generations. Children can, for example, "inherit" trauma reactions from their parents. This may include hearing direct stories about traumatic events. But it can also entail the passing on of dysfunctional ways that adults have used in efforts to deal with trauma.

In addition, it is important to address the connections between PTSD and traumatic brain injuries (TBIs). TBIs are injuries to the brain, skull, and scalp which impair a person's mental functioning.

The prevalence of TBIs in immigrant populations is not well-known. But it is thought to be substantial among refugees who have been exposed to war and other violence. In addition, there can be strong connections between TBIs and PTSD. Not surprisingly, a person can develop PTSD after having experienced head trauma. Both conditions also tend to involve similar symptoms such as problems with sleep, concentration, memory, and mood. TBI problems are further complicated if few (or no) medical services are available at the time of injury. It is important that patients track and share their complete physical trauma history when they do get medical help. That way the right treatment can be applied.

We cover various forms of treatment for PTSD later in this book. But there are a few things to consider first. For example, in our experience people with PTSD sometimes fear going to treatment, believing they will be required to tell the story of their trauma over and over again. There are treatments where that is the case, but such repetitions usually take place in settings where a person can be closely monitored to alleviate harmful reactions.

In our outpatient setting, we spend much of our effort thinking about and planning the future. There are five necessary components of the treatment of trauma: People need to feel safe, learn strategies to regulate their emotions, have social support (for example from friends and family), learn to understand their trauma experience better and find constructive ways to use that experience, no matter how bad it was, in their current lives.

> **Case example from Joachim Reimann:**
> Here is an example of a patient who was worried about having to tell his story over and over in therapy:
> Roughly ten years ago I worked with a patient who lost his wife and children in an airline disaster. He lived in a South American country at the time. Over

the course of psychotherapy, his symptoms improved, and we completed treatment. He was well-educated and ultimately obtained a good job in another part of California that was over 100 miles away. Then, in March of 2014, I received an unexpected call from him. That was when Malaysian Airlines flight 370 disappeared. The news coverage of this event was constant for weeks. You could not turn on the TV without getting the latest update. Because of the similarity between this disaster and his own experiences the man's symptoms flared up again. My initial thought was that, given how far away he now lived, this man should get a local psychologist to help him. But he did not want this saying that I already knew his story of trauma and he did not want to repeat that with a new therapist.

The story had a good ending; this patient ultimately did very well. But his reaction is a useful example of how a current, similar disaster to one previously experienced can stir up bad memories in people with a trauma history.

A final note: Over the course of our practice, we have encountered people who, at first glance, seem to just have an angry disposition, who respond to even minor problems with rage, and who appear to have substantial character flaws. They may also come in with a variety of diagnoses that were given by other doctors. But when we fully explore their history, it turns out that they have experienced major psychological trauma. As previously described, people who flee war, crime, and other threats to life in their country of origin (as well as in their travels) are often subjected to traumatic events and this becomes an important consideration with some immigrant groups. As psychologists with expertise in PTSD in immigrant populations, our job is to look beyond anger and emotional issues to the underlying factors, like trauma, that can cause reactivity.

ACKNOWLEDGMENTS

Many people have directly or indirectly shaped the content of this book. Our editor Ms. Leslie Schwartz helped us find the right style for you, the reader. She also asked important questions about our topics that we had not thought of otherwise. In addition, we are grateful to Mr. David Wogahn and Ms. Manon Wogahn from AuthorImprints who guided us through the many complex pieces involved in publishing this and other books in the *Immigrant Strides* series.

We appreciate our past collaborations with researchers at San Diego State University's Graduate School of Public Health. This particularly includes Drs. Gregory Talavera and John Elder. We also wish to acknowledge the friends and colleagues who worked with us on various projects over time. Most centrally, these include our friend and partner, Dr. Harve S. Meskin, Co-Founder of the Group for Immigrant Resettlement and Assessment (GIRA) as well as Dr. Mehboob Ghulam, Dr. Fouad Beylouni, Ms. Maria Elena Patiño, and Ms. Aida Amar. In addition we appreciate our work with leaders in the local East African communities, particularly Mr. Ahmed Sahid, President and CEO of Somali Family Service of San Diego and Mr. Abdi Mohamoud, President and CEO of the Horn of Africa organization.

Most importantly, we wish to thank our many patients and clients who shared their life stories with us over the years. They cannot be named here due to confidentiality regulations. But their experiences are at the heart of both this book's content and our motivation to write it.

ABOUT THE AUTHORS

 **Joachim "Joe" Reimann, Ph.D.** was born in Berlin, Germany. His family immigrated to the US when he was 10 years old. At present Joachim is a clinical psychologist and President of the Group for Immigrant Resettlement and Assessment. He has a long history of working with immigrant communities and is a former Board Chair for Somali Family Services of San Diego. While previously on the adjunct faculty at San Diego State University's Graduate School of Public Health, Joachim received grant support from the US Office of Minority Health, the National Center for Minority Health Disparities, the Hispanic Centers of Excellence, and the California Endowment. His work focused on a number of areas in behavioral medicine. These included type 2 diabetes, tobacco control, and colorectal cancer. As such, Joachim's research has been published in *Diabetes Care*, *The Diabetes Educator*, *Social Science & Medicine*, *Ethnicity & Health*, the *American Journal of Preventive Medicine*, and other outlets. In addition to a clinical focus, Joachim's doctorate has an emphasis area in Organizational Psychology. Consequently he has been part of various organizational development efforts

and has held administrative positions in government and the private sector over his career.

**Dolores I. Rodríguez-Reimann, Ph.D.** was born in Piedras Negras, Mexico. Her family immigrated to the US when she was 15 years old. A bilingual & bi-cultural (English/Spanish) psychologist, Dolores has worked with immigrant and refugee populations for many years. Specific venues include private clinical practice, past contracted services through Survivor of Torture International, and funded research. At present, Dolores is an executive with the Group for Immigrant Resettlement and Assessment. While an adjunct faculty member at San Diego State University's Graduate School of Public Health, she received grant and contract support through the National Heart, Lung & Blood Institute (NHLBI), the National Cancer Institute (NCI), and the US Office of Minority Health. Her research on public health related issues has been published in *Ethnicity & Disease* and the *Journal of Immigrant Health*. Dolores has also served in multiple organizational leadership positions over her career.

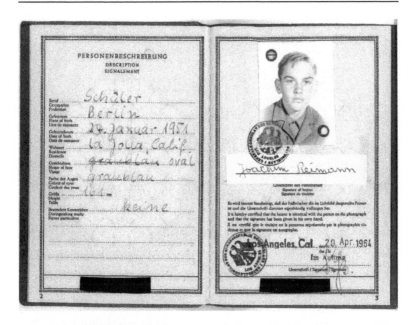

ABOUT THE COVERS

Upon viewing our planet Earth from space, astronaut Neil Armstrong has been quoted as saying "it suddenly struck me that that tiny pea, pretty and blue, was the Earth. I put up my thumb and shut one eye, and my thumb blotted out the planet Earth. I didn't feel like a giant. I felt very, very small." Others have noted an increased sense of connection to other people and the Earth as a whole. In short, astronauts have had the privilege of seeing our planet from a distance and come to recognize what humans share as opposed to what divides us. We believe it is important to remember these insights when we talk about immigration.

The 2023 film "A Million Miles Away" about real-life Mexican American NASA astronaut José M. Hernández includes the line "Who better to leave this planet and dive into the unknown than a migrant farm worker?" We cannot say it better than that.